on track ...

Gerry Rafferty

every album, every song

John Van der Kiste

SONICBOND

sonicbondpublishing.com

Sonicbond Publishing Limited
www.sonicbondpublishing.co.uk
Email: info@sonicbondpublishing.co.uk

First Published in the United Kingdom 2025
First Published in the United States 2025

British Library Cataloguing in Publication Data:
A Catalogue record for this book is available from the British Library

ISBN 978-1-78952-349-2

Typeset in ITC Garamond Std & ITC Avant Garde Gothic
Printed and bound in England

Graphic design and typesetting: Full Moon Media

Follow us on social media:
Twitter: https://twitter.com/SonicbondP
Instagram: www.instagram.com/sonicbondpublishing_/
Facebook: www.facebook.com/SonicbondPublishing/

Linktree QR code:

Acknowledgements

My thanks are due once again to Kev Hunter for his invaluable help in delving through his considerable archive of 1970s music papers – largely *Melody Maker* – and sending me relevant material; to Ian Herne and Eoghan Lyng for bringing to my notice several online articles and other items I would've missed otherwise, and for illuminating discussions on various aspects of Gerry's career; to David Belbin, Paul Jones, Julian Littman and Andrew Wild, all of whom have helped with advice and answering various questions.

As always, I am also indebted to my wife, Kim, for her support during my writing and research. It was she who mentioned several years (and intervening books of mine) earlier that Gerry Rafferty might be a suitable subject for future work. Last but not least, thanks to my ever-supportive publisher, Stephen Lambe, and the editorial team at Sonicbond.

Acknowledgments

on track ...
Gerry Rafferty

Contents

Introduction

As the title indicates, this book is a detailed look at the music of Gerry Rafferty. While a certain amount of biographical fact is necessary to put everything into perspective, I have deliberately avoided some details that were eagerly lapped up during his last years by certain sections of the news media.

All songs reviewed throughout these pages were written by Gerry Rafferty unless stated otherwise. For the sake of completeness, I have given track listings and details for the first Humblebums album, but for reasons of space, I have not described each song in depth, as Gerry was not involved. On the second and third Humblebums albums, I have focussed on the Rafferty songs and merely listed the others.

As a singer-songwriter and musician in two bands, in a duo and as a solo performer, Gerry Rafferty had a roller-coaster career as a performer in the British music industry for some four decades. Some maintain that he was the finest singer-songwriter Scotland ever produced. Always known for his uncompromising refusal to bow to the unwritten rules of a precarious profession, he was a staunch individualist, perhaps never quite as successful as his talents suggested he ought to be. Yet, he remained uncompromisingly true to himself and, in the process, left behind an astonishing catalogue of work. This included two immortal, much-loved songs that became top-ten hits (for himself and subsequently for other artists), both of them ironically inspired by and recalling in stark terms some of his decidedly unglamorous experiences in the business. For Gerry was one of those people who adored creating and performing music, but hated having to wade through the mire involved in selling it in a cut-throat environment to his audience.

Gerry Rafferty was born on 16 April 1947, the third son of Joseph – a miner and lorry driver who had emigrated from Ireland – and Mary Rafferty (*née* Skeffington). Mary had worked at a weaving mill. There were two elder brothers, Jim and Joe, and they lived at a council house in Underwood Lane in Ferguslie Park, a district in Paisley. The name would later be placed firmly on the musical map when the second Stealers Wheel album hit the shops.

Joseph, an alcoholic, was often physically abusive to his wife and sons. While the two elders were deemed big enough to give as good as they got, Mary dragged little Gerry around the local streets on Saturday nights so they would not be at home when her husband returned drunk. They would wait outside in all weathers until he'd fallen asleep to avoid a beating. More than once, she told her youngest son that if it wasn't for him, she would leave. Years later, he reminisced that his father's unhappiness and failings overshadowed their childhood. He said there were 'lots of unhappy times spawned from when I was a kid'. As for his father, 'His vision of the world was extremely narrow. It was an incredibly hard life'. Joseph's saving grace, as well as a great gift to his son, was his rich knowledge of Irish and Scottish traditional songs, which, on his better days and nights, he loved singing to the family, though he was tone deaf and physically deaf as the result of a punctured eardrum, and not always in tune. The music was one interest he shared with Mary, who also sang, 'She Moved (Moves) Through The Fair', being one of her favourites. The boys learned many of their parents' favourite songs by heart, traditional tunes and numbers like 'The Mountains Of Mourne': 'almost semi music-hall stuff that was written at the end of the last century, but which has its place'. From the age of around four or five, Gerry was especially intrigued not just by the songs themselves but by his awareness that he and his brothers weren't quite singing the same notes. When he asked why they were singing a slightly different tune, they told him they were singing in harmony.

More contemporary sounds later became just as influential. Like many children of his generation, he was soon enthralled by Elvis Presley and Little Richard. Years later, he recalled going into a fish-and-chip shop as a boy of nine, and 'Heartbreak Hotel' suddenly came on the radio: 'I'd never heard anything like *that* before. That's my most overpowering memory of being affected by rock 'n' roll.' He also loved Lonnie Donegan, The Vipers and skiffle and played his copy of 'Rock Island Line' to death. Many years later, he said he could see it was 'a very primitive, popular music form, but it gave an opportunity to working-class kids – who had no musical education – to sing simple songs with simple instruments'.

Going back further in time, he also developed a passion for music of the inter-war years, particularly Cole Porter, Jerome Kern and George Gershwin. 'The majority of the great songs are sad love songs, and that suits me fine'. His daughter Martha later added that it went back even further, from the hymns from Gerry's Catholic upbringing, such as the work of Ravel, to Frank Sinatra 'and that era of performance and production – he really aimed for that kind of polished, professional sound – that really spoke to him'. Being of Irish-Scottish blood with a Scottish upbringing, in later life he would say that he had absorbed the best of both musical cultures.

He attended St Mirin's Academy, a Catholic senior secondary school in Paisley, also attended by Joe Egan, who was two years his junior, and John Patrick Byrne, seven years older. Joe would play a regular role throughout much of Gerry's career, while John subsequently became, in turn, an artist, designer, printmaker, playwright and screenwriter. He also did much to encourage Gerry's musical aspirations, not least by lending his banjo to his friend Jim Rafferty, who asked to borrow it, as his little brother wanted to teach himself a Cliff Richard tune. Another school contemporary was John Reid, who would subsequently become the manager of Elton John and Queen.

Joseph died in 1963, and Mary survived him by nearly 40 years. With the main breadwinner gone, 16-year-old Gerry left school to take a job and help to support the family. For some time, he worked in a butcher's shop, a shoe shop, and as a social-security office clerk: menial jobs only meant to be short-term while he set about preparing himself for a career in music.

Early Days And The Fifth Column

To the Rafferty family, influences of traditional song and the diverse melting pot that stretched from 20th-century classics, the Great American songbook and early rock were added to those of the beat boom that electrified Britain around the time Gerry left school. But he refused to regard them as something that swept everything else aside like a Damascene conversion.

> There's so much bullshit talked about rock 'n' roll. It's easy looking back at 30 and saying, 'Yeah, when I was nine, that changed my life'. It didn't change my life, you know? There you are, someone at school, only a child, and there's so much stuff to go through. Rock 'n' roll was only one part of it.

1963 also marked the beginning of Beatlemania, and soon after that, Bob Dylan became the favourite of everyone looking for songs with more lyrical depth. The fusion of both styles would inspire many a teenager to pick up an acoustic guitar, get together with like-minded souls and form local bands who would find artistic fulfilment and supplement their day-job income from the weekend gigs at local dance halls. Their repertoire was mostly the usual diet of current and recent hits, especially Beatles and Rolling Stones songs. At length, some of them would also begin writing their own material.

One such band from Paisley was The Sensors, their vocalist being Gerry's old schoolmate Joe Egan. When they needed a new rhythm guitarist who could also share vocals, Gerry applied and duly joined the ranks. Joe and Gerry had long been fans of The Everly Brothers and realised that they, too, could follow Don and Phil's example by singing in harmony. This discovery was the beginning of a partnership that would endure, albeit intermittently, for many years. Gerry would sometimes resort to novel ways to get time off from the shoe shop. One day, he arrived at work covered in bandages, claiming he had been involved in a dreadful accident. Duly given sick leave, he returned home, removed the bandages and went to a group rehearsal.

After The Sensors disbanded, Gerry and Joe joined more-established outfit Maverix, with Rab Sinclair on lead guitar, David Storrie on bass and Dennis Bell on drums and vocals. For some months, they had a regular gig at the Pavilion Ballroom, Strathpeffer. It was probably here that they caught the eye and ear of an A&R man from EMI's Columbia label, who heard some of their original material and thought they had a distinctive sound. In the autumn of 1966, they entered the recording studios to record what would be their only single, released in November 1966.

The Fifth Column

'Benjamin Day' (Egan/Rafferty/Bell) (2.57)/**'There's Nobody Here'** (Egan/Rafferty/Bell) (2.29)

The A-side, with Gerry on lead vocal, told the story of Benjamin Day, a hawker who carried a bag full of 'Strange things for sale, straight from a fairy tale/Like an amethyst ring or a puppet on a string'. According to the EMI press release that accompanied promotional copies of the single, the song's inspiration was an Indian pedlar they'd given a lift to in their van one day. He seemed such a fascinating character that they had to write a song about him. Not knowing how to spell or even pronounce his name, they decided that Benjamin Day sounded rather effective.

With gently picked acoustic guitar and unobtrusive organ interwoven between the verses and chorus, charming vocal harmonies and imaginative use of minor chords, the atmosphere suggests a strong flavour of Paul McCartney, Paul Simon and even The Byrds. The B-side, with Joe on lead vocal, was a more punchy song with something of a nod to The Beatles' 'No Reply' – a young man looks forward to a rendezvous with the love of his life, goes to her house, rings the bell, knocks on her door, but finds she has left. Both songs suggested a talent ready for nurturing, but interest never spread beyond their home territory. Radio airplay and chart success eluded them, and the group soon disbanded.

As a one-off release that has so far been neglected by compilers of 1960s obscurities, the original 45 is now highly sought-after. At the time of writing, a major online record dealer advertised a demonstration copy in excellent condition for £195, saying that in almost 40 years of trading, it was the first they'd seen.

Writing credits were given on the label. According to later sources, including an article from the Paisley local press around 2000 and an interview with John Byrne, he co-wrote both songs with either Gerry or Joe, possibly both.

Returning to the press release, between them, Fifth Column had already written about 35 songs, which were destined to remain unheard or reworked for future use by the two main members who would go on to greater things. Almost the same melody of one, the very Beatle-ish-sounding ('A Hard Day's Night' era) 'Time Is Like A God', later uploaded on Youtube, with strong harmony vocals, would appear in 'Sign On The Dotted Line' on Gerry's first solo album.

The Humblebums

After Maverix and The Fifth Column had become history, Gerry joined the dole queue and returned to the Paisley folk scene. One day, he was enjoying a pint or two in the pub with fellow folk singer Danny Kyle, who told him that Billy Connolly – 'an amazing character' who played banjo in local duo The Humblebums 'and looked like Wild Bill Hickok' – was coming to join him shortly. Billy duly walked in. Also present were a pub pianist and Joe Egan, so the latter and Gerry took little persuasion to get up and sing an Everly Brothers number. Then Billy performed his song, 'Saltcoats At The Fair', and brought the place down. They immediately warmed to each other, though Billy thought there seemed something rather strange about Gerry, who was four years younger than him and looked like 'the kind of guy you'd expect to see hanging around in the darkest corner of a library'.

A few nights later, Gerry went to a Humblebums gig at the Orange Hall, Castle Street. When Billy and his musical partner – guitarist and mandolin player Tam Harvey – came off stage, Gerry told them how much he'd loved their set and asked if they would like to come back to his flat for a few beers. His real motive was not just to offer them hospitality but to seek a sympathetic ear or two for his songs, some of which he played. As Billy listened, he was amazed, his initial reaction being, 'Are they really his?'. Gerry was initially wary of this extrovert who, he said, 'looked like the Wild Man of Borneo', but at the same time realised this could be the break he needed. At their next meeting in the Scotia Bar at Glasgow – another favourite haunt of folk musicians – Billy formally invited him to join as a full member, and two became three.

The Humblebums had just released their debut album, *First Collection Of Merry Melodies,* on the Transatlantic label. The single 'Saturday Roundabout Sunday' was about to follow. What had briefly been a trio, or a quartet if their bassist Ronnie Rae was included, soon reverted to a duo. Tam realised that both men had much in common despite their very different qualities and personalities, and there wouldn't be a place for a musician who didn't write songs, so he stepped down.

Live performances were a simple affair for Billy and Gerry. They travelled light with a banjo and an acoustic guitar, usually for a fee of £100, cash-in-hand after the gig. Most of their early shows were around Scotland and the north-east of England, notably appearances at a folk club at The Rex Hotel, Whitley Bay – co-run by singer-songwriter Alan Hull, later of Lindisfarne – and occasionally further south. These alternated with the recording of a second album. On *The Humblebums* – or *New Humblebums* according to the label and back of the sleeve – Gerry proved himself to be the dominant creative force. He wrote seven of the songs, leaving Billy with four, alongside their version of the old World War I music-hall song 'Good-Bye-ee'.

Both knew their strengths and their limitations. Billy was a born entertainer and raconteur, while Gerry was the painstaking songwriter hiding behind his guitar. Billy readily admitted that Gerry was very good for him: 'He was a real musician, he knew and felt music, a bass player, with a lovely sense of harmony, as well as a great guitarist. I knew tunes and how to play them, but that was where my musicianship ended'. Billy acknowledged that he could be 'flashy' but was just not in the same league and recognised that his talents were best suited in other directions. Gerry, he said, 'was a musician, and I'll never be one of them'.

In many ways, their personalities were complete opposites: one the ultimate funny man, and the other the sensitive folkie. Billy's opening quip on stage that he had used on gigs with Tam was retained: 'Hi, we're The Humblebums, and I'm humble'. Yet they complemented each other well, had a similar sense of humour and soon became the best of friends. When Billy married in 1969, Gerry was his best man. Gerry knew that they'd instantly 'recognised something good in each other'. Billy, he went on, had a gift for getting people to respond instantly, while Gerry's lay 'in seducing people by singing, which is a much slower process'. One of them 'shocked people into listening by offending their sensibilities', which created a platform for the other to come forward and sing. It was a marvellous combination but with an edgy balance.

Moreover, Gerry wasn't always the intense introvert of popular belief. With his wicked sense of humour, it was his idea that, on wet Saturdays, they would walk the shopping streets of Glasgow looking for elderly ladies to scare. As they put up their umbrellas, he would 'accidentally' collide with them, shout and hit the pavement, taking a glass eye from his pocket and letting it roll, much to their horror. He was also an inveterate phone prankster, making hilarious calls with a straight face to unsuspecting victims. And when they were in Germany, he would seek out phone directories to look for people called Hitler. They never found one.

The partnership survived for nearly three years, long enough to record and release two albums that sold to a dedicated following without troubling the charts. At the same time, there were three singles – 'Saturday Roundabout Sunday'/'Bed Of Mossy Green' (both written by Connolly) in April 1969; 'Coconut Tree'/'Her Father Didn't Like Me Anyway' (both Rafferty) in August 1969, and 'Shoeshine Boy' (Rafferty)/'My Apartment' (Connolly) in March 1970.

First Collection Of Merry Melodies (1969)

Personnel:
Billy Connolly: vocals, guitar, banjo
Tam (Tommy) Harvey: vocals, guitar, mandolin
Additional personnel:
Ronnie Rae: bass
(Uncredited: other instruments)
Produced by Bill Leader
Record label: Transatlantic (UK)

Release date: February 1969
Running time: 29.13
All written by Connolly unless stated otherwise.

The Humblebums' debut album, recorded and released long before their paths had crossed with Gerry, was an enjoyable if unexceptional collection of, indeed, merry melodies that, for the most part, showed Billy taking inspiration from traditional folk and bluegrass. Several of the songs are credited to him, and the uncredited ones are presumably traditional. 'Little Blue Lady' is a brisk ragtime-come-skiffle romp with kazoo that could almost be an old Leadbelly tune covered by an early incarnation of Mungo Jerry. 'My Dixie Darling' was an old tune from Alvin Carter of Carter Family fame, the uncle of Johnny Cash. 'Why Don't They Come Back To Dunoon' and 'Salt Coats At The Fair' were more-or-less comedy songs, but undoubtedly sounded better in a live environment, and, as they say, you had to be there. Watching the young Connolly deliver them in a small folk club would've been a treat indeed, but on record, there is little to distinguish from so many other similar albums of the time.

'Why Don't They Come Back To Dunoon' (King: authorised parody, Connolly) (4:12)
'My Dixie Darling' (Carter) (2:32)
'Now I Feel So Old' (1:59)
'Give Me A Little Of Your Time' (2:06)
'Salt Coats At The Fair' (3:06)
'Victory Rag' ('Victoria Rag' on the label) (Uncredited) (1:39)
'Will You Follow Me' (1:58)
'Little Blue Lady' (1:46)
'Travel Away' (1:45)
'Come Drink My Wine' (3:24)
'Cripple Creek' (Trad. arr. Connolly) (1:58)
'Close Your Eyes' (1:21)
'Windy & Warm' (1.27)

The Humblebums (1969)

Personnel:
Gerry Rafferty: vocals, guitar, piano
Billy Connolly: vocals, guitar, banjo
Ramsbottom Brass Band: brass
Conductor: Norman Walmsley
Arranged by David Palmer
Produced by Bill Leader
Record label: Transatlantic (UK); Liberty (US)
Recorded at Sound Techniques, London; Railway Hotel, Ramsbottom, Lancashire
Release date: September 1969
Running time: 31:59
(Sometimes called The New Humblebums, as per the title on the back of the sleeve and UK record labels.)

Musically, The Humblebums Mk I had been pure folkies, faithful enough to accommodate the purists who might look askance at anybody wielding a guitar and suspect either of them might possibly – shock, horror – turn into a wannabe rock-'n'-roller, another Beatle or Elvis. With Gerry taking Tam's place, the folk-pop transition took over. Gerry's influences – almost a musical and lyrical synthesis of the Fab Four and Dylan – helped take the group in a more mainstream direction. So did the arrangements of David Palmer, their equivalent of George Martin, whose recruitment of additional musicians enriched the sound and broadened the appeal beyond the strict parameters of folk.

No individual players were credited on their first album, although the sleeve acknowledges Palmer as arranger and also the presence on the final track of the Ramsbottom Brass Band, conducted by Norman Walmsley. The arrangements are the icing on the cake, especially touches of strings and woodwind that sound not far removed from contemporary material by The Move and Honeybus. The album also marks the start of a recurring characteristic: a charming naïf-style painting by John Byrne on the front cover, showing Billy and Gerry flanked by a rabbit and a lion in the manner of a portrait by turn-of-the-century French artist Henri 'Douanier' Rousseau. 'Patrick' (as John signed himself) illustrated several more of Gerry's album covers throughout his career and painted designs for Donovan's *H. M. S. Donovan* and The Beatles' 'White Album', the latter initially rejected but used later for the compilation *The Beatles Ballads*.

'Look Over The Hill And Far Away' (3:39)
The collection opens with a charming song featuring Gerry's voice and acoustic guitar, accompanied by French horn, flute, pennywhistle and woodwind. There's an air of mystery in the lyric, which tells of a lonely young man at the windowpane, evidently looking out across the hill and beyond,

awaiting the reappearance of his loved one who has gone missing.

'Patrick' (2:19)
To acoustic guitar, woodwind and flute, Gerry sings a touching little letter set to music by John 'Patrick' Byrne, 'My primitive painter of art', his lifelong friend who illustrated the sleeves of so many of his albums, as well as the front of one of Gerry's Martin acoustic guitars with a portrait of him reclining in a landscape alongside animals, birds, flowers and a human skull. (The instrument was eventually bequeathed to his granddaughter Celia). The singer recognised that the artist was a skilled exponent of the Primitive style of art, producing sophisticated and richly detailed pictures in the style of the naïve school that flourished particularly in France in the early 20th century.

'Rick Rack' (2:48)
Gerry swaps his guitar for piano to deliver a delightfully childlike song of dreams of ambition, in which he contemplates all the things he could be when he grows up – an engine driver, a deep-sea diver, or a carpenter so he can fill his house with the things he's made. Dreams may come and dreams may go, while he sits beside the road watching a train coming down the track.

'Her Father Didn't Like Me Anyway' (4:32)
Undoubtedly Gerry's best song on the album, and the longest by almost a minute, is this touching, bittersweet track inspired largely by the character of his future father-in-law. A few descriptive lines paint the story of the brief love affair. His girlfriend always wanted more from him than he could give, and the coat he gave her still lies on the bed, as does the book he gave her that she never read.

When he was playing with The Sensors and The Maverix at a dance hall, Gerry met and fell in love with Carla Ventilla, a 15-year-old apprentice hairdresser from an Italian family in Clydebank, near Glasgow. In their early days together, she took him home to meet her father, who clearly cared little for the 'scruffy, itinerant, down-at-heel musician' that had captured her heart. Much of the courting apparently took place at the home of the more sympathetic John Byrne. Yet there was a happy ending in that in 1970, they married and remained husband and wife for 20 years, even if her father didn't fully approve. The unpromising son-in-law-to-be was to become friends with Mr Ventilla. The latter was a charming man in many ways, Gerry admitted towards the end of his life, and he even grew to like the song, 'but, unfortunately, he didn't have much sense of humour'.

About ten years later, he said this song and 'Patrick' were the best of his early songs – 'the most real things I did' – certainly the most personal. The baroque arrangement of woodwind instruments, reminiscent of songs like the then-recent Honeybus hit 'I Can't Let Maggie Go', adds immeasurably to the charm. He was to revisit it on another album a quarter of a century later.

It was soon recorded by several little-known British folk acts and some 20 years later by Shane McGowan and the Popes. Among the first converts on the other side of the Atlantic were Kenny Rogers and the First Edition. Their 1972 album *Backroads* (never issued in the UK) included this song and the opening song on this collection under the abbreviated title 'Look Over The Hill'.

'Please Sing A Song For Us' (2:42)
Songs on the theme of *Mr Music Man, come and entertain us and we'll all join in* are part of a long-standing tradition, but this was by a mile the most commercial tune on the album. It's dominated throughout by a jaunty, even naggingly infectious piano hook that must've qualified it for potential hit single status. Once heard, surely never forgotten.

'Blood & Glory' (2:27)
A mention of armies fighting a running battle from Nebraska to Seattle suggests a reference to the Battle of Seattle in 1856, which started with an attack by native American tribesmen. This is unusual among the Humblebums' catalogue in that Billy's banjo picking can be heard quite prominently in places alongside Gerry's guitar.

'Coconut Tree' (1:57)
This is a whimsical tune about a man escaping from a nagging wife who took all his money. Now, he's found a more peaceful life sitting beneath a coconut tree where nobody will ever find him. The backing is mostly Gerry's acoustic guitar, augmented with unobtrusive lead, bass and percussion.

Non-Rafferty tracks (all Connolly unless stated otherwise)
'Saturday 'Round About Sunday' (2:32)
'Everybody Knows That' (2:59)
'Joe Dempsey' (1:45)
'Silk Pyjamas' (2:32)

'Good-Bye-Ee!' (Bob Weston/Bert Lee) (1:55)
This last was a popular music hall song in Britain during World War I.

Transatlantic Records and its offshoot, Big T, comprised a small company with limited promotional resources and only minimal chart presence. Under the auspices of a larger organisation, they might've helped to establish a better foothold in the marketplace. Yet they had two champions on BBC Radio 1. 'Shoeshine Boy' was a favourite of Kenny Everett, and 'Please Sing A Song For Us' of John Peel, but no hits were forthcoming. The former received a glowing review on the singles page of *Melody Maker* (28 March 1970) from Bob

Dawbarn, who praised the 'good, unpretentious Rafferty song nicely sung and played against an attractive 4/4 beat ... there's a pleasant air of relaxation about the whole thing'.

While The Humblebums still had quite a modest profile outside their home patch, some of the media were beginning to take notice of the factor that made them stand out above the swathe of folk acts on small specialist labels: the songwriting talents of their newer member. Gerry was flattered to find himself being called 'One of the new breed of singer-songwriters'. Being spoken of in the same breath as James Taylor and Joni Mitchell was praise indeed.

Open Up The Door (1970)

Personnel:
Billy Connolly, Gerry Rafferty: vocals, guitar
Jimmy Tagford, Terry Cox: drums
Bernie Holland: guitar
Barry Dransfield: violin
Arranged by Harry Robinson
Produced by Bill Leader
Record label: Transatlantic (UK), Liberty (US)
Release date: June 1970
Running time: 42:35

By the time the duo wrote and recorded *Open Up The Door*, they were moving even closer towards the mainstream. On a Radio 1 session recorded in February 1970, they were augmented by Daryl Runswick on bass, Bernie Holland on guitar, and Mike Travis on drums. Bernie – a member of fellow Transatlantic band Jody Grind – also played on the album.

As far as the Billy/Gerry albums and singles were concerned, it was still almost a case of never the twain shall meet. Each of them sang their own songs on record and on stage, often with no input from the other. The odd couple appeared on the same stage, the same vinyl, and there it ended. Rarely, if ever, did they pretend to be a Scottish equivalent of the Everly Brothers or Simon & Garfunkel. In his memoirs *Tall Tales And Wee Stories*, Billy later remarked that Gerry 'didn't share very well musically'. Even if they recorded something together, the latter would sometimes return to the studio on his own, add further contributions and erase anything on the tapes from Billy. Even on stage, the latter would sometimes get ready to join him on the next song, only for Gerry to turn to him and say he was going to do this one on his own: cue Billy's footsteps off stage for the next three minutes.

'I Can't Stop Now' (4:37)

'You know I'm in too deep and I can't stop now', Gerry sang – a simple love song thanking the love of his life for having opened up the door to him. After a subdued verse with restrained drums and bass, the chorus positively soars, enhanced by strings. It's very close to the kind of richly orchestrated pop that fellow Scotsmen The Marmalade specialised in at around the same time.

'All The Best People Do It' (2:51)

This gently self-defensive lyric was sung from the point of view of someone who is reproached as being out of touch and retorts that his opposite number is 'Tryin' hard to be so cool/But you will always be the fool'. But with the sturdy piano and some unobtrusive lead guitar, it was one of the most catchy songs on the album. Whether it was a coded message from its writer to his musical partner, let the listener decide.

'Steamboat Row' (2:04)
Gerry often recalled how when he was a child and his dad had had a few pints, he would reminisce about when he lived in a row of miners' cottages known as Steamboat Row at Inkerman, Paisley. This touching little tune with a light backing of acoustic guitars and percussion was to resurface later on a Stealers Wheel session for Radio 1 and on their second album.

'Shoeshine Boy' (3:12)
The single that caught the ear of Kenny Everett on Radio 1 had potential hit written all over it, and just a little more airplay could've made it one. The sprightly tale of a kerbside bootblack working downtown for a menial wage while dreaming of Saturday night when he can take his lady out dancing is set to an irresistible tune and a more-forceful-than-usual guitar solo, given added colour by organ, with an interesting finish that sounds almost out of place. The song also attracted the attention of Jonathan King, who produced and probably sang backing vocals on a version by child-actor-turned-singer Simon Turner in 1972. The two were like chalk and cheese. King loved Gerry's music but once described him as the most impossible artist he'd ever worked with. Gerry may have found that King personified everything contrived and artificial in the music business, which Gerry disliked so strongly.

'Keep It To Yourself' (3:07)
This is one of the most complex of Gerry's early lyrics. The narrator is lamenting the departure of a woman who 'only loved me when the weather was fine'. There's an interesting scenario in the next verse when he catches the subway train, takes a seat next to the door, spots a man that he's sure he's seen somewhere before, and they look away from each other as the train slows down. It's rather like two or three unfinished short stories in one. It begins with a bustling bluesy guitar riff, gathers pace with the drums, and a few effective bursts of strings and flute add some drama to the gaps between verses.

'Song For Simon' (2:18)
The identity of Simon is anyone's guess, but this guitar-backed tune is a humorous portrait of how people can suddenly find themselves in very changed circumstances in a moment. A man fast asleep in bed suddenly finds himself on the chimney top; a woman playing her banjo has a huge crash and finds herself up in the sky, and 'young Joseph Egan' (sounds familiar) is cleaning his car one morning when a giant comes out of the bonnet and carries him away. 'Who knows what the day will bring' goes one repeated line, and would give its title to a later CD anthology of Gerry's early work. The verses read like a nursery rhyme. Gerry admitted that it was 'kids' stuff', choosing this and 'Keep It To Yourself' as his favourites on the record.

'My Singing Bird' (3:04)
Songs about birds seeking freedom were very much in vogue around this time: The Beatles' 'Blackbird', Leonard Cohen's 'Bird On The Wire' and Elton John's 'Skyline Pigeon', to take but three: add this one to the list. Seated at the piano with no additional musicians to be heard, Gerry offered a charming ballad – an ode to a winged creature (which could be a metaphor for a love about to leave), asking to stay with him for one more night, as in the morning she would be far away.

Non-Rafferty Tracks (all Connolly)
'My Apartment' (2:47)
'Open Up The Door' (3:21)
'Mary Of The Mountains' (3:00)
'Mother' (2:55)
'Oh No' (2:12)
'Harry' (2:57)

Neither member ever saw The Humblebums as anything other than a short-term project. In the summer of 1970, while still recording *Open Up The Door*, Billy told Andrew Means in *Melody Maker* that there was 'nothing surer' than a parting of the ways: 'Groups should split. Otherwise, they become a bore. What we thought was making us a very original group is, in fact, pulling us apart. We have so many different influences'.

When The Beatles spectacularly disintegrated in 1970, there seemed to be an unofficial hunt for, if not exactly, a *new* Beatles, then someone to fill a vast hole. Gerry appeared almost resentful of the persistent comparisons coming his way. In the same interview with Andrew Means, he emphasised that the Fab Four's influence on them (or rather him) was now diminishing: 'I am much more mature and so is my music. I know what I want to do now'. Ralph McTell – another contemporary British singer-songwriter on the Transatlantic roster at the same time – was not alone in telling the press that Gerry sounded 'a bit McCartney-ish', implying mild criticism. Some of Gerry's songs that people insisted were in that vein had been written some years ago, possibly for future singles by The Fifth Column, if Columbia had ever considered taking up an option on any more.

The duo-that-was were becoming a band, leaving the intimacy (and also sometimes the stifling old-school nature) of folk clubs behind in favour of larger venues and the festival stage, where the label felt that exposure on a wider scale would sell more records. More often than not, they felt out of their depth in such surroundings. One of the worst bookings that they played was the weekend Yorkshire Folk, Blues & Jazz Festival in mid-August 1970, which only lasted two days instead of three because of bad weather. The Humblebums had the dubious privilege of opening the show on Friday evening, sharing a bill with Elton John, The Pretty Things, Georgie Fame and

Atomic Rooster. They might've worked better on the following day's programme, playing alongside Ralph McTell, Fairport Convention and Sandy Denny's new band Fotheringay. The Humblebums' drummer valiantly played on with an umbrella held over his head as the rain was coming through the flat stage roof while workmen were trying to drill holes in the stage to let the water out. At least they were given some credit by one reporter who said their Scottish humour 'and lively folk songs took away some of the gloom'.

Later that month, after the Jazz-Bilzen Festival in Belgium alongside Screaming Lord Sutch, Cat Stevens and Badfinger were followed by another appearance as a duo again opening for Atomic Rooster (an ill-assorted pairing if ever there was one), the duo decided they'd reached the end of their road. Gerry was wearying of Billy's jokes and anecdotes becoming ever longer, up to 20 minutes at a time, while Gerry was having to shoehorn his own two-minute songs into the act when he could. In October, they pulled out of a gig at Sunderland Polytechnic because – according to the following statement – 'As members of the group could not guarantee to the management's satisfaction that future engagements would be fulfilled, in the interest of audiences and promoters, no further dates are being accepted for the group by Transatlantic'. They had, in fact, gone back to their homes in Scotland to reconsider what looked like an uncertain future together or else a future apart.

Early in 1971, they played their last contracted date. Gerry was philosophical about the parting of the ways, and for him, it was the end of 'three wonderful years'. Yet it had always been a peculiar combination, a pairing of 'The raging extrovert, and me as the fairly shy introvert'. As they were moving in different directions, they had run their course and were jaded with the folk club scene, which Billy said had become little more for them than 'some crowd of idiots singing 'The Wild Rover''. For him, the last straw was 'a real nightmare of a gig at a workers' club in Methil, Fife. It was all hot pies and bingo and guys going 'Boo', and we stomped off without finishing our set. We should never have ventured within five miles of the bloody place, but we knew then that was our final gig together'.

Gerry's version of events was a little different. Talking to Colin Irwin in *Melody Maker* eight years later, he thought that the differences between them had been over-emphasised, and anybody who shared a stage with someone like Billy could hardly not come across as introverted. He himself felt quite self-contained, and it was his idea to form a band rather than be part of a duo. He felt Billy was rather scared of going back to the folk clubs out on his own, 'and I don't think he forgave me for that'. He'd been content to participate in the straight-man/funny-man routine, but he also soon came to hate the audiences they were playing to – 'folk clubs in front of guys with Aran sweaters and 'A few pints chaps and we're all chums together'. Hahaha, rugby songs and all that shit. Billy always seemed quite comfortable with that kind of setting, but I despised it'.

Both of them were also scathing about how pretentious and false some of the other performers were. While working in the folk clubs, they were highly suspicious of 19-year-old folk singers from Dublin and Glasgow singing what he called 'old men's blues' from the repertoire of people like Big Bill Broonzy. Gerry could never take them or their music seriously, as he further elaborated:

> But all these people seemed to have so much more credibility because they were being so very ethnic. It was the same bullshit thing you always get, you know? I'm here thinking, 'Where have they heard all *this* stuff?'. Here's me, I've been listening to Cliff Richard for ten years – I haven't heard *this* on Saturday Club. My experience was not at all of being ethnic about it, but just of soaking up a whole lot of things through the radio and records, through jukeboxes.

Gerry Rafferty Solo, 1971

The Humblebums were still contracted to Transatlantic as a duo. Having stockpiled a large collection of original songs, Gerry was intent on forming a new band but still owed the label one more album. To some extent, both projects could be taken on board simultaneously. He'd befriended Rab Noakes, another guitar-playing Scottish singer-songwriter, who would be much more of a kindred spirit musically and personally. Rab had also been a regular at the Rex folk club sessions, Whitley Bay, and their paths crossed even more closely at a pre-show get-together on the afternoon of The Humblebums' first major Glasgow concert in the City Hall, where they'd been invited to sing a couple of songs. 'Later, as we were packing up to go, we engaged in a dressing-room rendition of The Beatles' 'In My Life', and a lifetime friendship was born. He was a month older than me, so we were total, shared-experience soulmates in the sense of being post-war offspring of the 1950s and 1960s'. Gerry had far more in common as regards personality and musical aspirations with Rab than with Billy, and it was hardly surprising that Gerry and Rab should gravitate towards each other before long.

In February 1971, *Melody Maker* reported in its 'Focus On Folk' section that Gerry, Rab and Roger Brown (an American guitarist and songwriter who'd been based for some years in Europe) were forming an acoustic group, with a long-term possibility of expanding into a five-piece to include keyboards, drums, bass and guitars. They planned to begin rehearsing in April, with a view to starting live work in May but had no intention to record yet. As Roger was unable to obtain a work permit in Britain, he had to bow out, effectively reducing them to a duo as far as live work went. Nevertheless, he continued to play with them on an informal basis and contributed to Gerry's forthcoming solo album.

It was either at one of their first sessions or at the pub where they were kicking around ideas for the right group name. Gerry had always liked the word 'wheel' and its connotations, and one of them – probably Roger – immediately suggested Stealers Wheel. It sounded too good not to use.

Gerry's house at Tunbridge Wells was effectively the birthplace of Stealers Wheel, was where they used to rehearse and was 'consistently alive with singing, strumming and writing'. Rab also released his debut album, *Do You See The Lights?*, in 1970. Both men slipped comfortably into a much more equal working relationship than there had ever been in The Humblebums. Rab later recalled how they'd play for hours together by day, then sit up all night just chatting, singing and writing new songs, and spoke for both of them when he called it 'the launch of a cherished partnership' and said how everything fell into place as they 'suddenly found themselves hitting all the right notes'. Rab said, 'I love to sing, especially with other people, and it wouldn't be a lie to admit that my best companion in that was Gerry'. Between them, they had a large collection of songs, some their own, some old favourites from yesteryear and from musicals. Sometimes, there were parties where they were joined by friends and family, including Gerry's elder brothers Jim and Joe. 'There would always be a couple of songs from the trio in the most gorgeous sibling-driven harmonies. 'Island Of Dreams' was good, but the most astounding song was from *Seven Brides For Seven Brothers:* 'I'm A Lonesome Polecat'.'

For Gerry, it was a case of leaving one duo to form another. Stealers Wheel, who looked and sounded much more like a unit of two equals from day one instead of two individuals who were plainly chalk and cheese, played their first gigs in late spring 1971 at small venues in Scotland. Their debut was at the Caley Cinema, Edinburgh, on 30 April. In *Melody Maker,* John Gibson noted that both performers 'sounded good for each other – Rafferty's light, almost fragile delivery contrasting effectively with the relative sonority of his partner in the vocals'. He found the guitars 'intelligent without ever being obtrusive' and their material 'impressive in its simplicity'. The only fault was that their material lacked 'a stark change of pace and mood'. Songs like 'Can I Have My Money Back?' and 'Rick Rack' had undeniable charm, 'but there was nothing to relieve the lightness, the wistfulness, the poignancy of it all'. Despite this, he was sure they wouldn't be 'standing still' and were 'going to make a tremendous impact on the folk scene'.

Two months later, on 5 July, they appeared in London, supporting Lindisfarne at the Marquee Club. Gerry later told *Zigzag* that these performances were done largely out of financial necessity. Ironically, this date would probably be more lucrative for Rab, in the early years of what would be for him a profitable connection with the Geordie quintet on the verge of major success. They had already recorded his song 'Turn A Deaf Ear' on their debut album *Nicely Out Of Tune* the previous year and would include his 'Together Forever' on their forthcoming *Fog On The Tyne*: one of the UK's best-selling albums of 1972.

Meanwhile, Gerry had his contractual obligation album to complete for Transatlantic. Rab, Roger and Joe duly rallied to the cause by contributing backing vocals. The cream of the day's session players – including veteran jazz violinist Johnny Van Derrick, who had played on recent albums by Elton John and Mungo Jerry; keyboard player Alan Parker of Blue Mink and CCS fame; and Gary Taylor and Andy Steele, who had been bassist and drummer with The Herd – were also recruited. Hugh Murphy – a member of the record company team who was drafted in as producer – realised that the more basic folk sound, as favoured by Humblebums producer Bill Leader, didn't bring out the full potential of Gerry's songs and was given *carte blanche* to help the singer aim for a more ambitious piece of work. There are little bits of late-period Beatles, Kenny Rogers-style country, jazz-pop *à la* Alan Price Set and others, and hints of Bonzo Dog Band music hall. By turns sardonic, tender and cheerfully commercial without being irritating, it was one of the first albums in that peculiarly British self-effacing, unashamedly whimsical pop-meets-folk style, predominantly acoustic with subtle enhancements from strings and brass, also personified by the likes of Al Stewart and Clifford T. Ward. Moreover, it marked the beginning of a musical partnership that was to be rekindled later in the 1970s, with only occasional interruptions until Hugh's death in 1998. Noakes later recalled with amusement that at one of the first get-togethers of the Stealers Wheel quartet, the album was almost being recorded in secret, and Gerry would 'nip behind the sofa to finish a lyric'.

Can I Have My Money Back? (1971)

Personnel:
Gerry Rafferty: guitar, vocal, piano
Joe Egan: backing vocals
Rab Noakes, Zed Jenkins, Alan Parker: guitar
Roger Brown: guitar, backing vocals
Gary Taylor: bass, backing vocals
Rod King: steel guitar
Hugh Murphy: backing vocals
Tom Parker: Hammond organ, harmonium, harpsichord
Tom Lasker: piano
Henry Spinetti, Andy Steele: drums
Johnny Van Derrick: violin
Produced by Hugh Murphy
Recorded at Morgan Studios, London
Record label: Transatlantic (UK), Blue Thumb (US)
Release date: October 1971
Running time: 40:23

'New Street Blues' (2:59)
A few seconds of muffled chat ('Do it on the microphone, thank you, Gerald') lead into some sharp stabs of brass, organ, lead guitar and piano rhythm. Stuck at home, our hero decides to go downtown and look up a friend with whom he can talk or drink the night away – a theme Gerry returned to on another 'street' song with more success a few years later.

'Didn't I?' (3:42)
Love, doubt and seeking reassurance are the main themes in this charmingly simple song. 'Didn't I tell you we could make it as long as you believed in me?'. Paisley meets Nashville, with a little help from country-style steel guitar alongside the usual acoustic picking, bass and drums.

'Mr Universe' (2:43)
This jaunty, gently humorous song with a Bonzo Dog Band air was inspired by reading a bodybuilding advertisement in a comic and took the form of a plea from a seven-stone weakling sick of having sand kicked in his face to be turned into somebody different. A man's voice announces grandly that 'You can have a body like mine', and lively piano with Beach Boys-style vocal harmonies made this one of the more accessible songs.

'Mary Skeffington' (2:31)
Mary Skeffington was Gerry's mother's name, and he used the melody of her favourite hymn, 'Sweet Sacrament Divine', as the intro when writing a song for her as he urged her gently to go to sleep 'and make believe that you are

just a girl again'. We can assume that Mary heard the song, as she lived to be 95, passing away around 2000. Gerry remained proud of it, later saying he thought it 'a nice little song', and was happy when people told him it was one of their favourites. 'I draw less from the past these days, but I've certainly drawn on the past in many songs'.

'Long Way Round' (4:49)

The longest number on the album was a song of travel, with an element of mystery or an unexpected twist. A traveller looks across the water, travelling to the other side where someone is waiting for him. He gets onboard a ship in stormy weather on a rough sea, and a stranger sits next to him. It turns out to be his brother, who later walks away without knowing where he's going. A convoluted, unfinished story is given colour with a backing of predominantly piano and organ, supplemented by some subtle touches of bass and lead guitar towards the end and striking vocal harmonies. Anyone familiar with Procol Harum's seafaring epic track 'A Salty Dog' might wonder whether it had any influence on this song.

'Can I Have My Money Back?' (1:51)

Inspired by a recurring childhood memory from Paisley, aged around nine or ten, Gerry regularly went to an old flea-infested cinema known as The Bug Hut. Films were always at the mercy of a half-drunk projectionist, and patrons' viewing pleasure of *Superman* or *Flash Gordon* was often spoiled by the film suddenly breaking down. If it wasn't fixed, the box office would be besieged by youngsters demanding a refund. So goes verse one. Then we're introduced to the politicians, who do nothing to alter the status quo of one law for the rich, another for the poor. It's sung to a jaunty skiffle rhythm with fiddle and pennywhistle throughout, and after the final verse, Johnny Van Derrick's sprightly fiddle dance finishes it all off. It gave Gerry his first modest taste of single-chart success, reaching number 70 in Australia.

'Sign On The Dotted Line' (Rafferty/Egan) (2:34)

A listen to the unreleased Fifth Column song 'Time Is Like A God', as mentioned above, will remind us that Gerry was not one to waste a good tune. The dream of the aspiring rock 'n' roller seeking a career and coming up against the money man with the big cigar was an inspiration that Gerry and Joe would have good reason to revisit later on. Trading a relatively untroubled existence playing guitar in a small bar for a life controlled by someone who pretends to be a Starmaker, signing on the dotted line and then wishing he'd stayed at home instead, is the theme, and might've in part served as a metaphor for the future of the young 20-something songwriter recording his first solo album. Some unobtrusive yet effective brass touches, striking multi-tracked vocals and harmonies make this another of the more commercial tracks, bringing Dean Ford's vocal and again the style of

Marmalade to mind. Like 'Shoeshine Boy', Simon Turner recorded this on his 1973 album.

'Make You, Break You' (3:29)
Imagine a mid-period Beatles outtake with a slightly funky rhythm, underpinned by forceful piano with a catchy tune, and that sums up the spirit of this track well. There's a bit of a John Lennon feel about the lyric, a sly putdown of a woman who's not quite all she seemed at first – butter wouldn't melt in her mouth, and 'Every time I see you look in a mirror/I can tell that's who you really are'.

'To Each And Everyone' (2:46)
A keyboard intro – probably a harmonium – leads into a bittersweet song of farewell. The narrator says goodbye to everyone around him, who could be his friends or family: 'I know it's been fun, but we're living a lie'. Mid-tempo with more crisp keyboards in the instrumental break, the song ends on a rather lovely and definitely Beatles-inspired chord.

'One Drink Down' (Rafferty/Byrne) (2:50)
The one song in Gerry's solo catalogue co-written by the artist who painted so many of the album sleeves was a plaintive country waltz, with violin prominent in the backing. A son has married an unfaithful woman who suddenly leaves without warning, and the only solution to an old problem is to be found – we learn in the opening line – in 'Rafferty's Bar'.

'Don't Count Me Out' (3:49)
Inhabiting similar territory to 'Make You, Break You', this is a mid-tempo song but of lesser quality and probably the weakest track on an otherwise excellent album. Lyrically, it's rather slight, as he begs his friend not to tell him to drink too much and that it'll be the death of him: 'Don't count me out'.

'Half A Chance' (4:26)
One of only two songs to pass the four-minute mark, this is about going out on the town to an evening show. The entertainment includes singers, Lily the generously endowed stripper and 'Billy with his big banjo', and to use a *cliché*, a splendid time is guaranteed for all. The song goes through a few dynamic changes, with touches of music hall, a few seconds of soft jazz guitar, and most distinctively of all, piano-led sections that sound very much like The Beatles' 'The Fool On The Hill'. Though not immediately the most commercial song, it's probably the most adventurous.

'Where I Belong' (2:03)
The album finishes with a fairly short and rather personal-sounding song, Gerry just accompanying himself on piano, with no vocal harmonies or any

other instruments. Lyrically, the message is bleak, about finding it harder to get through each day. The vague hope of being where he belongs is really the force that keeps him going. It makes a rather downbeat ending to an album that, in several other tracks, provided humour and a good share of instantly commercial fare.

Bonus Tracks (*Who Knows What the Day Will Bring?* anthology (2019))
'So Bad Thinking' (Egan/Rafferty) (3:22)
Originally the B-side to 'Can I Have My Money Back?, there's a slight jazz feel with the mellow lead guitar and piano. Love has gone wrong in the lyric; she's never going to see the light, and it's 'so bad thinking about it' that he can't sleep at night. This also appears as a bonus track on some 21st-century CD reissues of the album.

'Mary Skeffington' (Overdubbed version) (2:31)
This was the original recording, with the unnecessary addition of what sounds like a horribly bland synthesized accordion and equally irritating percussion in places.

It was released as a single in 1978 (B-side 'Shoeshine Boy') by Logo Records, who had acquired the Transatlantic catalogue and were keen to cash in on the success of 'Baker Street'. Not having been consulted, the artist himself was unimpressed.

'Who Cares' (Demo version) (4:58)
This is the first of three rather different versions of the same number in the Rafferty catalogue. The 'demo version' is relatively laid back, with the melody playing mainly over two alternating chords. Nowhere does the exact title appear in the lyric, the closest it gets being the line 'Do you really care?', along with phrases like 'Do you ever stop to care?' and 'Have you found a friend in Jesus?/Have you found a friend at all?'. Later on, the piano, drums and partly wordless vocals (falsetto at times) take a more scat direction.

'Bernard' (2:45)
This is an early version of 'Mr Universe', or rather a run-through of the tune, with what sounds like placeholder lyrics made up on the spur of the moment but the same backing track. At one point, Gerry calls out to the other musicians, 'Okay, slow part'.

'In Loving Memory' (3:32)
This instrumental is a slow and relaxed piece with acoustic and electric guitars and a shuffling rhythm on drums and piano. Rather like the preceding number, it was probably intended as a backing track or musical sketch to be given lyrics at a later stage.

'Make You, Break You' (Alternative version) (2:47)
This sounds a little less polished than the finished version, although the differences are slight and it has a fadeout ending.

'Don't Count Me Out' (Alternative version) (3:53)
As with the previous track, there are minor alterations in the phrasing, but with little to tell it apart from the finished item.

'Mr Universe' (Alternative version) (2:42)
Once more, there's barely any difference from the officially released track, apart from the lack of guest singers.

'Martha' (2:13)
Named after Gerry's daughter, this was evidently either a work in progress or an idea that would be subsequently reworked and assimilated into another song, with wordless vocals and mainly bass and drums.

'Way Of Knowing' (4:29)
A slow instrumental or backing track, mainly lead guitar and drums.

'Who Cares' (Finished master) (5:07)
About ten seconds longer than the demo version, this is similar apart from the more-or-less improvised vocals – sometimes wordless, sometimes following the have-you-found-a-friend-in-Jesus? theme and sounding as if performed by someone else with a rather louder, less melodic voice than Gerry. Occasional stabs of brass also appear. The song underwent further changes before being recorded in 1973 by Stealers Wheel for *Ferguslie Park*.

Seven years later, after Gerry's second solo album, *City To City*, had become a major global success, Hugh Murphy (by then not only Gerry's co-producer but also his official tour sound supervisor) told Fred Dellar for *Sound International* what a pleasant experience the sessions had been. Gerry came along with some tunes, some of which had no words, and Hugh told him he knew some good players that would be available.

> We made this album for £1200. I got people who I thought were the best, and we did about two-thirds of that album one Saturday. However, we weren't too happy with a couple of things, so we pleaded with Nat (Joseph of Transatlantic) and got another 300 quid out of him, which meant that the budget went up to £1500. We went into Sound Techniques because it was folksy, homey and comfy, and with the help of engineer Jerry Boys, we did three more tracks. That album got great reviews, and when we went on tour recently, we found that everybody seemed to know every tune from it.

Reviewers indeed loved the album, with Penny Valentine showing particular enthusiasm (*Sounds*, 6 November 1971):

> The vastly underrated Mr Rafferty comes up with a splendid album worth time and money in anyone's language. One of the best British songwriters and musicians to emerge in the past couple of years, Rafferty has the kind of talent that demands your attention. His songs are wryly gentle, his voice clear and evocative, but the real strong point he's always held is in his melodic content, which is so strong it brings back memories of McCartney at his best.

Roy Hollingworth of *Melody Maker* called it 'a pure gem of English [sic] contemporary music' and likewise declared himself an admirer:

> Thirteen songs, all penned by Raff, and each one as varied and as imaginative as you'd wish for. His music is very very good, and no matter how much electricity and orchestration he goes for at times, there remains something as natural and unpretentious as being glad and letting people know it. He's also moody, and there are a couple of melancholic lengths that are syrupy and delicious.

In the US, *Billboard* called Gerry's songs 'rich and memorable with an undeniable charm that will definitely see him into the album and very possibly singles charts soon'.

The release of *Can I Have My Money Back?*, sometimes called the first *de facto* Stealers Wheel album, was preceded by the appearance of the title track as a single, with 'So Bad Thinking' on the B-side. With shades of things to come, Gerry put little effort into promoting it beyond recording a session for Radio 1 and a two-song appearance on BBC TV's *The Old Grey Whistle Test* in December ('Can I Have My Money Back?' and 'Didn't I?'). There was no question of any immediate live dates, let alone a tour, either solo or with a band. Nevertheless, his reputation as a songwriter was beginning to spread beyond a small circle of more discerning radio presenters and music journalists. Within a few months, 'Mary Skeffington' had been covered on the debut solo album by Allan Clarke (who had temporarily left The Hollies), *My Real Name is 'arold* (which also included his version of the Joe Egan song 'Walpurgis Night'), and on Olivia Newton-John's LP *Olivia*.

Gerry always remained very proud of the album. After he resumed his solo career later in the decade, he said he still enjoyed playing several songs, particularly the title track.

Meanwhile, the Stealers Wheel era was just opening. For a while, it was temporarily Gerry and Joe Egan, as Rab had amicably decided to leave and return to a solo career, mainly playing the folk clubs. Joe proved to be a worthy replacement, as he and Gerry had – in the latter's words – struck up 'the most amazing relationship': an affinity that had endured since the Fifth Column days and one they were glad to rediscover. Gerry: 'There really was something special between us. The blend of our voices was astonishing.'

Stealers Wheel

In December 1971, Stealers Wheel made their radio debut. The first BBC session comprised three songs ('Sing A Song For Us', 'Steamboat Row' and 'I Get By') on a Radio 1 concert supporting Lindisfarne, introduced by John Peel. Having been an admirer of Gerry's work with The Humblebums, Peel was more than ready to give his support to the new outfit. He said Gerry 'has one of my favourite voices' – a quote the A&M press office readily used in press kits sent out with the first album a few months later.

With another gig supporting Lindisfarne at Newcastle City Hall that same month, Gerry and Joe needed additional musicians to bring out the best in their growing repertoire. In interviews, Gerry had made no secret of his intention to get back into an electric band, in a situation similar to that of The Maverix (except this time with original material), or alternatively continue where The Fifth Column had left off after one single. Writing and playing 'slow melodic things' as part of The Humblebums was very frustrating 'as I really wanted to get up on stage and blow'. That was something he looked forward to with this new band. In an interview with Mark Plummer of *Melody Maker*, Gerry made plain his dissatisfaction with the contemporary folk scene:

> (It's) so tight, it's almost like one big family. There are some aspects of it I did like, but the fact that anybody playing an acoustic guitar is a folk artist, brought me down most. When I think of folk, there are two things that come to mind. I think of real traditional music that I love and the people like Bert Jansch, The Incredible String Band and Steeleye Span: people who have broadened their outlook. It's really the middle. The Clancy Brothers and The Spinners (the Liverpool quartet) are good examples; to me, they epitomise everything that is bad about the folk scene.

It was a prescient remark. Three musicians who would later appear on several of his albums and on stage with him during some of his all-too-rare gigs in Britain and Europe, namely Liam Genockey, Julian Littman and Pete Zorn, would later also be regular members of Steeleye Span.

Meanwhile, the next to join Stealers Wheel was drummer Peter Clarke, formerly of Liverpool band The Escorts. He brought with him guitarist Paul Pilnick (the two having played together in a band with Apple Records artist Jackie Lomax) and bass guitarist Iain Campbell, who'd been in bands at the Star Club in Hamburg at the same time as The Beatles in their early days. Stealers Wheel made their radio debut at a concert opening for Lindisfarne on 2 December 1971 (broadcast five days later and introduced by John Peel) with two of Gerry's early songs – 'Please Sing A Song For Us' and 'Steamboat Row' – and a new one by Joe called 'I Get By'.

Two months later, they recorded four songs for Radio 1, including Joe's 'José', 'I Get By', 'Get On The Right Track' and 'Mary Skeffington'. Later that year, Clarke and Campbell left, to be replaced by bassist Tony Williams and ex-Juicy Lucy drummer Rod Coombes. Further Radio 1 work followed, mostly featuring songs from the first album. Later, in 1972, they signed with the A&M label, which bought Gerry out of his remaining contractual commitments with Transatlantic for £3,000. The new company originally planned to offer the production job either to Gus Dudgeon or Tony Visconti but subsequently chose Jerry Leiber and Mike Stoller, renowned for their work with the likes of Elvis Presley, Peggy Lee and The Drifters. To have these two stalwarts of late-1950s and early-1960s music, looked like a privilege indeed.

Stealers Wheel (1972)

Personnel:
Gerry Rafferty: guitar, vocal
Joe Egan: keyboards, guitar, vocal
Paul Pilnick: guitar
Tony Williams: bass
Rod Coombes: drums
Guest musicians:
Iain Campbell: bass
Luther Grosvenor: backing vocals, guitar, lap steel
(Uncredited: saxophone)
String arrangements by Richard Hewson
A Leiber-Stoller Production
Record label: A&M
Release date: November 1972
Charts: UK: did not chart, US: 50, Canada: 25, Australia: 44
Running time: 33:26

The band's debut album found Joe the more dominant of the partnership, as he wrote or co-wrote eight of the ten tracks, and Gerry only six. Credited as executive producers, comments from others suggest that Leiber and Stoller were not particularly hands-on in the recording process, though the latter played harpsichord and was responsible for the horn arrangements. The engineers involved should've taken more of the credit and gotten at least a mention on the sleeve. Geoff Emerick, who'd worked closely as George Martin's assistant on many of The Beatles' records, was at the helm for some of the backing tracks before handing the job to John Mills, another engineer at Apple Studios, where the album was recorded. George Harrison was also at the studio around the same time, recording part of his album *Living In The Material World*. He dropped in briefly on sessions on the grounds that Apple was his company and he 'should be staying on top of things', but only out of curiosity as a casual observer.

No matter how the division of labour panned out, working relations between the senior American partnership and the two much younger Scotsmen and bandleaders were not that harmonious. Joe, who was a little more overawed than his musical comrade in arms by their good fortune, said some years later that both producers really made them feel at ease 'and were great to work with, I thought anyway'. That may have been Joe's view, but Stoller said he found Gerry difficult to work with and seemed to look on them with distaste, even hostility. Stoller also thought the band's work ethic was lacking, especially in their over-reliance on brown ale and Scotch to keep them going and their hasty departure out of the doors at pub opening time. Moreover, Gerry always seemed wary of success, and once they'd achieved that longed-for hit, he appeared suspicious of what they'd created and no longer really liked it.

John Byrne's striking sleeve images of each group member with their heads superimposed on the body of an animal or bird continued his tradition of illustrating the records Gerry was involved in. This time Byrne had discreetly woven the name Stealers Wheel into the picture several times. Trying to detect the names on anything other than the original LP record cover – except for the one in large lettering at the bottom – is almost impossible.

'Late Again' (Egan/Rafferty) (3:11)
The first track was also the first to be released as a single in Britain, in October 1972, a month ahead of the album. It attracted little airplay and failed to chart, but for some people, it was their first introduction to the band on vinyl. With its warm harmonium sound at the start and a melody which seems to hint at nothing so much as an old hymn, it's a tantalising, beautiful sound. Rhythm guitar is mixed well back, making keyboards and drums the most prominent instruments until the saxophone break halfway through. As would often be the case with their songs, a beguiling tune masked an expression of angst, in this case, dissatisfaction with a woman ready to reproach her partner for his regular lateness. He knows that when she gets back, she'll grumble that he's been absent too long, and he wonders why he returns, but 'There's always something there that keeps me hanging on'.

Though it never charted, this and the subsequent track on the album were the only Stealers Wheel songs to remain in Gerry's live repertoire in his very few live appearances up to the final gigs in 1993.

'Stuck In The Middle With You' (Egan/Rafferty) (3:21)
This was the first single released in America, issued there in February, and became an instant hit, reaching number six while reaching number two in Canada. British chart success was yet to come. Persistence had its own reward, and the across-the-board appeal of the song was evident when rock critics praised it, *Sounds* calling it 'a cross between white-label Beatles and punk Dylan, yet with a unique Celtic flavour'. Paul Simon admired what he called with a smile 'the best Dylan record since 1967'. Tony Blackburn – at that time, the Radio 1 presenter the British weekly music press probably admired the least – made it his record of the week on his weekday breakfast show. Gerry's sardonic vocal sounded remarkably like a British Dylan, and the song was so infectious.

There was something of an irony in that a song that so mercilessly lambasted the music industry and bit the hand that fed it should turn out to be so successful and, in fact, become the only major hit the band ever had in their short history. The lyrics mockingly told the story of how A&M Records had thrown a launch party at the up-market Kings Road, Chelsea restaurant, the Aretusa, shortly after signing the band. They sat at a long table, 'like one of those scenes from the Last Supper', with about 50 people in attendance. There were musicians mingling with producers and, naturally, record company executives and their wives, and many a bottle of wine was emptied. It was easy to tell who was who from their attire. The musicians were in their habitual casual jeans and jackets, while the other men were in smart evening suits and the ladies in long dresses. Gerry had the misfortune of being seated between (or stuck in the middle of) two exceptionally boring label executives and their wives, none of whom seemed at all interested in talking about the music. Clowns to the left, jokers to the right, in fact. Two days later, he and Joe sat down and wrote the song in half an hour as the phrases just tumbled out, culminating in that immortal line. Rab Noakes, who'd also just signed to A&M for his debut album (including, inevitably, Gerry and Joe on backing vocals), recalled that the label boss seemed very aloof, and they all thought it seemed ludicrous that people there were talking about the band, but not to its members.

Before the story got out, others in the media were giving their own interpretations of the words. A particularly tongue-in-cheek theory came from journalist and radio presenter Charlie Gillett, who contributed a column to *New Musical Express* (*NME*) about it. In America, the Watergate scandal was just breaking and would lead to President Richard Nixon's resignation from office the following year. Gillett suggested that the lyric could almost be a verbatim transcript of a press conference in which a beleaguered Nixon was trying to defend himself.

Musically the song was one of their least complex, an infectious singalong beloved of the average guitarist as most of it was based around three chords in the key of D, with just a solitary fourth major chord of C near the end of the verse. That fourth chord apart, the main verses' basic chord pattern followed much the same as for a 12-bar blues.

Gerry always remained quite matter-of-fact about the comparisons drawn between Stealers Wheel and Bob Dylan and never minded it. He admitted that he and Joe's vocal inflections and phrasing were reminiscent of their hero, as were the subject matter and dark humour. The latter was not lost on future film producer Quentin Tarantino when he made the film *Reservoir Dogs* almost two decades later. Wanting a soundtrack based on 1960s and 1970s oldies, he successfully approached Gerry, through his management, for permission to use the song. The latter was given minimal information about the picture, merely that it was set in Los Angeles and that it would be violent. He didn't watch it for some time 'because it wasn't the type of film I normally go to see'. Later, he was told that the most gruesome scene was when one character had his ear cut off. After he saw it for the first time a couple of years later, in terms of cinema, he conceded that 'it worked incredibly well'.

'Stuck In The Middle With You' was the full title on the album label, 'Stuck In The Middle' on the UK sleeve and single. The UK sheet music used the full title, as did the UK press release, the US single and the album on the sleeve and label. To date, at least 60 cover versions have been released by such diverse acts as The Jeff Healey Band, Adam Faith with Roger Daltrey, Dennis

Waterman, Michael Bublé, Rick Nelson and The Stone Canyon Band, Leif Garrett, Susanna Hoffs and Keith Urban. The most successful (albeit a somewhat sugar-coated dance version) by Louise was a number-four British hit in 2001.

'Another Meaning' (Egan) (2:50)

As an introspective song about searching for the meaning of life and the uncertainty of knowing what to believe in, Joe pleads at one stage, 'Will someone please put on the light and make me feel alright?'. He ends on the rather doomy reflection that 'Every day gets a little bit harder'. Despite the almost fatalistic flavour, the general musical feel is quite sunny. Stoller wanted to introduce a Latin feel to the recording, provided, if possible, by a full Mexican band. As this proved to be impractical, he came up with the idea of playing one-note runs with dimes stuck in the strings of a piano, while Coombes added cowbells that gave a steel-band flavour. Subdued acoustic guitar and even a few touches of mandolin add to the texture.

'I Get By' (Egan) (3:11)

Stealers Wheel could never really be classified as anything but a soft-rock band, but on this B-side of the first single and a particular favourite when it came to recording Radio 1 sessions, they lurched remarkably close to hard-rock territory. Singing nonchalantly in the first verse about waking up too late to go to work and then taking the dog for a walk instead or about never being ready and bound to get there late (as in the first song), Joe sheds the British Crosby, Stills & Nash mantle and briefly heads for Rolling Stones or Free territory. There are also veiled anti-music business references directed to the man with his fancy cigar: 'I don't want no fast car'. At the same time, guitarist Paul Pilnick takes an all-too-rare opportunity to flex his muscles on some really loud, dirty guitar riffs and an equally powerful, gritty solo near the end.

'Outside Looking In' (3:48)

Something completely different had to follow the prior track. This song by Rafferty had a message of disillusionment similar to that of a number penned by Leiber and Stoller and a hit for Peggy Lee a few years earlier: 'Is That All There Is?'. It starts languidly, with thoughts of how 'It looked so good from the outside/I couldn't wait to join the crowd', so he took a trip down to the sea, only to find nothing there but sky and ocean. The key line is 'I'm never satisfied till I've been disillusioned'. Nothing is ever as good as it's cracked up to be – a reference to Gerry's pursuit of success in the music industry, perhaps, and maybe a feeling of how alienated he would feel once he'd hit the big time. Musically, it's laid back most of the way, with the occasional scream on the word 'alive', a few bursts of urgency on drums and guitar, ending in a scorching solo on the latter that perhaps fades a little more suddenly than it should. All in all, there's plenty of light and shade on a song that needs a few listens to appreciate to the full.

'Johnny's Song' (3:40)
This slow, restrained song combines introspection with advice to an old friend who has been 'taking it so hard' but has to keep moving, not letting things get him down and not swallow the lies of everyone around him who tells him he's doing fine. Perhaps it can be summarised in the line, 'Don't you know life's as good as being dead?'. There are several stops and starts, some concise but powerful blasts on the drums and jagged bursts of guitar, including a guitar solo at the end that again could've been allowed a little more time to breathe properly.

'Next To Me' (Egan/Rafferty) (3:35)
This song is so slow that it borders on an ethereal haze, with sweet electric piano and organ, swirling acoustic rhythm guitars, soft-shoe-shuffle percussion, bass so muted that it comes across as little more than an apologetic blur and a kaleidoscope of wordless vocals that take up almost the second half of the song. Such words as there are comprise just two verses, a semi-abstract musing on how 'Each day you try on a different person/Trying to find out who you really are'. Even the title is basically abstract, appearing nowhere in the lyric. The track is gentle and easy on the ear but tends to verge on the insubstantial.

'José' (Egan) (3:20)
What's this about – slave labour in the agricultural community? Again, the lyric is short, only comprising three brief verses. José is ordered to pick up his fork, turn the hay, get the job done, can't afford to rest, and that's as far as it goes. There's some promising guitar riffing that isn't really allowed to get up a full head of steam, and apart from the unfriendly lyrics, the whole thing sounds rather hurried or undeveloped.

'Gets So Lonely' (Egan) (2:52)
Two gentle but undeniably charming tracks conclude the album. Joe's tender, simple paean to loneliness when 'There's really nothing left to say' is accompanied by the soft velvet tones of an electric piano and more soft-focus vocal harmonies on the chorus. Again, one detects a McCartney influence hovering overhead.

'You Put Something Better Inside Me' (Egan/Rafferty) (3:40)
Keeping one of the album's masterstrokes till last, here comes the song that was the album's second British single, was played heavily on Radio Luxembourg but was never a hit and the one that Gerry later called one of his favourites among the songs he and Joe wrote together. Had it been

reactivated as a 45 in the wake of 'Stuck In The Middle', it might've received its due reward. Here, at last, is a note of optimism about the man who doesn't care at all and is busy going nowhere as nothing means nothing, and then he finds the right person. As others have pointed out, it could be interpreted as a song about faith as much as about love. The duo wrote one of their strongest melodies and a life-affirming message to go with it. Once more, restraint is the key on the backing – piano, acoustic guitars, a few lines of lead guitar curling around the gaps, a gentle touch on the strings and flawless vocal harmonies. It didn't go unnoticed at the time, and cover versions by Rod Stewart and Kiki Dee were to follow.

A remixed version with brass and additional strings appeared on a 1978 compilation album in the wake of Gerry's solo success. *Stuck In The Middle With You: The Best Of Stealers Wheel* was credited for the benefit of buyers with short memories or perhaps younger fans, to Gerry Rafferty and Joe Egan.

The title above is as written on the UK album sleeve and label. The UK single, released in February 1973, had 'You Put Something (Better Inside Me)' on the label, while the US album and single (which didn't appear until May 1974) had 'You Put Something Better Inside Of Me'.

Related Track

'Everyone's Agreed That Everything Will Turn Out Fine' (Egan/ Rafferty) (3:05)

The band's fourth (and only standalone) single had been recorded by all six members: Gerry, Joe, Luther, Paul, De Lisle and Rod. Released in the US in June, it peaked at 49. With a slightly abbreviated title, it appeared at home in August, and another appearance on *Top Of The Pops* at the end of the month helped it rise to 33.

The song didn't stray too far from the one and only hit. To some ears, it sounded more than a little like 'Stuck In The Middle', especially the instrumentation and handclaps that formed the basis of the eight-second intro. It was also surely one of the most sarcastic lyrics of its time. Lines like 'Don't ask any questions/You won't get an answer, oh no', and the implications of 'Everybody seems to have a good time/Nobody goes stepping out of line/Everyone's agreed that everything will turn out fine' can hardly have been lost on any but the most cloth-eared of music executives. It demonstrated Gerry and Joe's belief that rock musicians were being treated like naughty schoolboys and had to shut up and do as they were told – or at least until the final verse with its murky scenario of rolling in the gutter, throwing up their pride, bellyful of whisky, and so on. Moreover, the four members who'd just been given their marching orders must've regarded the title with some bitterness.

The group appeared on *The Old Grey Whistle Test* in November 1972, reprising the debut single 'Late Again' and 'I Get By', to mark the album release. A second Radio 1 session one month later comprised 'Late Again', their version of The Allman Brothers Band's 'Midnight Rider', 'Chevrolet' (presumably the Lonnie & Ed Young song) and 'I Get By'. In December and during the first few weeks of 1973, they promoted the album with several gigs around Britain. The first two singles ('You Put Something (Better Inside Me)' in February 1973 being the second) were favourably reviewed, though they never charted in Britain.

Gerry and Joe were ideal partners in the band, their voices harmonising to perfection until it sometimes sounded like one of them double-tracked. There were minor differences. Gerry usually sounded more laid-back with a tone somewhere between John Lennon at his most mellow and Bob Dylan, whereas Joe could easily be roused to sing in more of a growl if the song required him to as if he could give the likes of Free's Paul Rodgers a run for their money.

Like Gerry's first solo album, the group's debut was greeted with favourable reviews, though it never charted in the UK. One of the most supportive came from Bud Scoppa in *Rolling Stone*, 24 May 1973: 'Stealers Wheel can certainly be accused of theft. They make no attempt to hide their influences. But then, they've had the good sense to steal from some of the very best sources. Besides, imitation has always been basic to the pop process'.

There was one major complication. Gerry left the band shortly after the album was released and went back to his home in Scotland. Everyone else was mystified as to why he'd gone, the common belief being that he didn't want to go on tour in the US to promote the album. Joe, who had known him the longest and was the closest group member to him, was taken completely by surprise. Almost 40 years later, he was none the wiser. In the TV documentary *Right Down The Line*, he explained that they never spoke about it: 'He felt he had to do it at that particular time. But it wasn't a good feeling to be left to continue, to fulfil contractual engagements and all that kind of stuff; it was a nightmare. But we got on with it'.

In an interview with Michael Gray, that would appear in Gerry's 1978 solo tour programme, he explained what a difficult situation he'd found himself in:

> I was going through a very strange period in my life right then. I'd got married, had a child, I was 24, and one day, it was like I'd been living in a dream for six or eight years and suddenly woke up. It was a pretty scary kind of feeling. Perhaps I was on the edge of a nervous breakdown; that's how it felt anyway. I just had to get away, away from groups, managers, record companies, the whole thing. So, I picked up and moved back to Scotland to sort myself out.

At around the same time, he explained to *The Guardian*'s Stuart Wavell that the demands of the industry complicated things even further in that there was tremendous pressure for all of them to cash in on the record's success. 'It was like a roller-coaster being set in motion, and I suddenly realised I wasn't in control of my life anymore'. His brother Jim put it more bluntly: 'He didn't like being ordered around and told what to do'. Gerry was replaced by Luther Grosvenor, former guitarist with Spooky Tooth.

Evidently much in demand where Radio 1 sessions were concerned, they followed with a third in January 1973, playing 'Gets So Lonely', 'You Put Something Better Inside Of Me', 'Outside Looking In', and 'Here Comes The Queen', a single by Luther from his 1971 solo album *Under Open Skies*. A fourth session in June included 'Johnny's Song', 'I Get By', 'Late Again', and for the first time, a song logged as 'Everything Will Be Alright', presumably a mistitling of their forthcoming single and second of their three top-40 hits.

During the last weeks of 1972 and early 1973, the reconstituted group toured the album as support to David Bowie on his first national tour since becoming the most talked-about name in British music the previous year. Although it might've seemed like excellent exposure for them, the recently departed Gerry opined that it was the worst thing their management could've done, as the potential audiences were completely different from Bowie's. With Gerry having decided he was 'definitely finished with bands', he was considering writing more songs on his own and recording another solo album.

'Stuck In The Middle' was released in America in February, beginning its slow but steady rise up the American singles charts, and came out in Britain in April, proving to be third time lucky in Britain after two failures, and Gerry wondered what would happen if they were needed to appear on TV. As he had sung lead vocal on the track, any suggestion that Joe should have to mime to it seemed wrong. Nevertheless, a video for the song was made, with Joe the obvious (and only) choice to mime to Gerry's lead vocal. Shortly afterwards, one of the managers phoned to ask him 'to help out with the band', as they had a series of gigs lined up in Holland, and he agreed to return.

The record was given the coveted new-release spot on BBC TV's *Top Of The Pops* on 18 May, the first of its three appearances at fortnightly intervals as they watched it soar to a peak of number eight. A surviving clip of their performance shows them in the studio, Gerry looking very solemn whenever the camera catches him while Joe grins from ear to ear.

In spite of this, shortly before they were due to tour the continent, it was Joe's turn to announce that he was leaving the band. For the last few months, he'd had to shoulder all the responsibility of being the frontman, and he'd reached breaking point. Management and the record company were in despair until he relented and agreed to stay just long enough to play the Dutch dates. Gerry, therefore, returned to find himself playing alongside two members he hardly knew – Luther and DeLisle Harper, who'd replaced Tony Williams on bass. The band was briefly a six-piece, consisting partly of strangers recruited to fill the holes yet who had little in common, personally or musically. It was a very different outfit to the one Gerry had recorded the album with the previous year. He thought the live sound was awful. Luther was optimistic that everything would come together once they had the right equipment – in particular, the proper guitar pickups that they needed to play their quieter, mainly acoustic numbers properly. One person who attended a gig at Sunderland Polytechnic at the time posted on an online thread many years later, saying they were the loudest band he'd ever heard. As far as he could see, Luther was the frontman, and Gerry wasn't in the lineup at all.

There was also talk of sending them on tour in America to capitalise on the success of the single there, but that never happened. Yet it was too late to cancel the European schedule, and in Gerry's view, the hastily reconstituted band was a complete shambles. When he discussed the matter with Joe, they found that Ricochet Management had been playing each of them off against the other, telling them various untruths. Determined to have a greater say from now on, they decided they would both stay. After the tour was complete, they planned to tell Ricochet that they intended to reduce Stealers Wheel to a duo and bring in session musicians to record the next album. After returning to England, there was a bitter argument with the rest of the band when they learnt that they were no longer required.

But it was not quite the end. A booking had been arranged for them at the Oxford University Ball, and when they tried to cancel it, the management threatened legal action. The band blamed Gerry, accusing him of returning and splitting them up and 'running off with Joe'. He and Joe met privately just before the show and had a few drinks because they knew what the atmosphere was going to be like later. On their arrival at the venue, the ticket collector asked who they were. When they told him, he accused them of lying. They ignored him and walked in. He attacked them and a fight ensued (also involving the man's father, who was collecting tickets as well) before it was sorted out. They arrived at the dressing room to find the rest of the band with arms folded, along with wives and girlfriends who'd come to give them moral support. There was a major row, and the gig itself – their very last – was a musical disaster.

Luther, who'd been sharing vocals with Joe in Gerry's absence, and drummer Rod Coombes, who'd joined before they recorded the album, were both particularly aggrieved at being dismissed. They said Gerry had caused a good deal of frustration and bitterness. All they wanted to do was promote the record on stage with a minimum of fuss, and once he'd left, they thought the group dynamic had settled down very well. When it was suggested that Gerry should rejoin, they thought the idea was ridiculous, as his departure had caused so much ill feeling. They said no, but on second thoughts, realised that if they accepted him back, they'd be able to reproduce the album much better on stage.

Meanwhile, Luther and Joe had jointly agreed to undertake writing songs for the next album, but the pressure of attempting to do so while on tour was too much for the latter. Gerry rejoined in time for their last dates in Holland, just as Joe was threatening to go. A period of intense confusion for the rest of the band and management alike only came to an end when, in Rod's words, Gerry and Joe 'got together and found each other again'. Luther said Gerry's return suggested great potential for them all, but he never gave them a chance. Joe and Luther had agreed to take two months off, sort out the equipment properly and resume live work after that, 'but Rafferty doesn't know where his head's at'. He felt he'd worked his heart out for nothing after playing his full part in a band that had promoted the single and made it a hit while Gerry was out of the band. Ever since, they were gradually getting everything right, and now 'Rafferty's just gone and blown it'. To Luther and Rod, Gerry's attitude seemed to be one of 'We've got a hit single, we don't need a band'.

Gerry and Joe held a press conference to announce their future plans. Stealers Wheel would definitely be continuing, with further recording in mind. At around the same time, Luther and Rod said that Gerry told them he wasn't interested in ever playing live again, something he flatly denied at the conference. He would welcome further gigs, but only if and when the band sounded good enough. (Years later, a comment on an online thread from a David Bowie fan who saw one of the first performances and had never heard the Stealers Wheel album opined that their stage performance was 'an aural battering'.) Otherwise, they were to confine their activities to making records. When Steve Clarke of *NME* interviewed Joe in June, a reference was made to American concerts being scheduled for November, but this never came to anything.

Some years later, Humblebums manager Mick McDonagh said that Gerry probably played more shows with Billy Connolly than in the rest of his career put together. He also spoke to Gerry in the dressing room at *Top Of The Pops* and was astonished when he said he wasn't going to tour but intended to 'knock it on the head'. Mick observed that *that* was the point when 'the self-destructive gene kicked in', adding that he thought Joe was blissfully unaware of such intentions. Others later in the same position would have similar experiences. When asked for his side of the story, Gerry said there was 'so much politics in the band and between band and management'. Their live performances were poor because there was too much distraction from interviews and other promotional activity; they lacked proper time for rehearsals, writing songs and creating the music, and everything seemed hopelessly rushed.

It was partly because of difficulties around this time that the misconception that Gerry hated playing live came about and hung around his neck like an albatross. According to his daughter Martha, he *did* enjoy being on stage and always had a great deal of respect for his fans: 'It was the machinations around the music business that he had a healthy distrust of'. Moreover, he felt ticket buyers were entitled to a professional show and that performers owed it to them to maintain the highest standards. He was a perfectionist in the recording studio and wanted to play their music properly on stage. If he thought Stealers Wheel sounded under-rehearsed and shambolic, as the one who originally founded the band, he had every right to say so.

Having proved their viability with one of the summer's most talked about singles and a transatlantic top-ten hit, the pressure was on for more.

Ferguslie Park (1973)

Personnel:
Gerry Rafferty: guitar, piano, mandolin, kazoo, vocal
Joe Egan: keyboards, guitar, vocal
Peter Robinson: piano, Hammond and pipe organ, synthesizers, chimes
Gary Taylor: bass, Minimoog
Joe Jammer, Bernie Holland: guitar
Andy Steele: drums, percussion
Chris Neale: harmonica
Corky Hale: harp
Steve Gregory, Chris Mercer: tenor saxophone
Mike Stoller: harpsichord, horn arrangements
Strings arranged by Richard Hewson
A Leiber-Stoller Production
Recorded at Island Studios, London
Record label: A&M
Release date: November 1973
Charts: UK: did not chart, US: 181
Running time: 39:17

Stealers Wheel recorded the second album as a duo with session musicians, some of whom were already familiar to them from earlier studio projects. Harpist Corky Hale was married to Mike Stoller, and sax player Steve Gregory's previous credits included The Rolling Stones and Georgie Fame. Following up on a debut that had spawned such a successful 45 was always going to be difficult. Gerry ruefully commented that, in some ways, it would be their downfall.

Two of his songs came from the Transatlantic era. One was a new recording of 'Steamboat Row' from The Humblebums' *Open Up The Door*, while 'Who Cares' had been recorded for *Can I Have My Money Back?*, sounding very different but never completed to his satisfaction. Some of the newer ones were partly written from bitter experiences, a reflection of what they'd been through with the band during those unstable early-summer months.

Ferguslie Park took its title from the sprawling Paisley housing scheme, which was more or less synonymous with urban deprivation in the 1970s. It was titled thus, Gerry explained, as they wanted 'to get as far away as possible from all the bullshit of the music industry in London. It reminded us of our roots. We were clinging ferociously to our roots. Our identity and our songs were formed in this town'. Several session musicians contributed, alongside strings arranged by Richard Hewson and horns by Mike Stoller. It emerged that the latter was the sole producer this time, at least in practice, despite what the album sleeve might say.

As if to try and break with their past, a new version of 'Everything Will Turn Out Fine' (again a shorter title) was recorded, given added urgency with heavier slide guitar and more forceful drums than the comparatively laid-back single. The album's second single, 'Star', proved to be more successful, even if one of their abiding memories of the song was having to promote it on the German TV show *Beat Club*. After hanging around the studio for several hours, they went on with their acoustic guitars to mime (or at best supply a live vocal to the backing track) to a bored-looking audience who looked like they didn't want to be there anyway.

Like the first album, the emphasis was on melodic folk rock. There was the occasional burst of aggression that teetered on hard-rock territory, but always with the tuneful harmonies of both vocalists.

John Byrne's outer and inner sleeve illustrations – which on this occasion extended to the vinyl label – portrayed the duo as farm labourers in charge of an absurdly swollen cow. It supported Gerry on its back, with Joe leaning against it, the former with a skull-shaped guitar (inspired by the anamorphic design in Hans Holbein's 16th-century painting 'The Ambassadors') against his shoulder, while the latter stood with an arm around the animal's neck. Surrounding them were numerous macabre birds and reptiles, recalling some of the nightmare visions of Dutch artist Hieronymous Bosch.

'Good Businessman' (Egan/Rafferty) (4:12)

A title like this should serve as a good warning of *Beware, vitriol ahead*. Here was a forceful rocking veneer of electric piano, saxes and a subtle reprise of the 'Shakin' All Over' guitar riff: listen carefully a third of the way through for that. It might've made your average rock fan loon around happily in time with air guitar after a couple of pints in the pub on the jukebox had it been issued as a single. The song itself was a no-holds-barred assault on music business professionals preoccupied with making money from complete unknowns as long as they played his game. A good businessman 'ain't in this business to be friends with you'. Bands got angry, dressed up their most incisive lyrics with a strong tune, decent playing and all the audio thrills at their disposal, and nobody except perhaps journalists and record buyers would notice.

'Star' (Joe Egan) (3:00)

The song by Joe that provided the group with their second and final top-30 entry was another self-mocking song aimed squarely at the non-day wonder of the business who would all too soon find himself a casualty of the built-in obsolescence syndrome: the *build 'em-up, knock 'em down* syndrome. It might've been about them, though Joe later had to defend himself against rumours that it was written about Luther Grosvenor, who'd adopted the showbiz name Ariel Bender and temporarily taken over guitar duties in Mott The Hoople. It was catchy enough to chart at number 25 in the UK and number stateside, with the rather chilling lines 'After all you've been through/Tell me what will you do when you find yourself out in the cold?'

being no deterrent for buyers; some jaunty kazoo and harmonica fills plus a break featuring jolly pub piano, sugar the pill of a bitter ode to disillusion and weariness, to perfection.

'Wheelin'' (Egan/Rafferty) (3:45)
With no sprightly tune as in the previous track to put a gloss on proceedings, this world-weary ballad painted a bleak picture of everything going wrong. It's all about people sitting up talking through the night, who thought they'd reached the end of their woes and then found everything going wrong again. The next day, they're standing onstage in front of a large crowd, and 'In the middle of a song/Everything was going wrong'. As a band who'd made one very good album and found it impossible to perform properly on stage, they had been there and done that. A sax break about halfway through gives way to a chorus that crossfades with a stately cacophony of chimes, akin to what sounds like an explosion in a museum of medieval clocks.

'Waltz (You Know It Makes Sense)' (Egan) (3:00)
A crossfade from the previous track takes us into a soft-shuffle ballad with an otherworldly, dreamlike atmosphere of pipe organ and fairy-dust sounds. Lines like 'There's no use sitting on the fence/When you know it all makes sense' suggest more skulduggery in the managerial department but in a less angry musical scenario this time.

'What More Could You Want' (Egan/Rafferty) (3:06)
There's no dreamlike atmosphere here as the anger resurfaces. A pattern has already started to emerge on this record, which is becoming almost akin to a concept album on the trials and tribulations of being an aspiring rock star. Sometimes, Gerry and Joe were resignedly accepting their fate as lambs to the slaughter, then in the next song, anger and defiance came through. Defending themselves with all the attack that wah-wah rhythm guitar and the odd angry solo can muster, they let rip this time. The target was clearly a management that was taunting them – 'Just get on out there/Don't look so serious/You've got a brand new Telecaster/What more could you want?'.

'Over My Head' (2:53)
This is one of several Gerry songs from around this time where he manages to paint a broad, introspective picture in very few lines. An all-night conversation comes to an end with the dawn of another day and a walk outside to watch the sunrise. Unlike some of his other numbers, there's a feeling of positivity and hope for the future as he looks to the sky and feels the joy of being alive: 'Don't let it go, don't let it slip away'. It has a slow tempo and a dreamy tune with stately piano chords on the intro, giving way to ethereal organ and strings (courtesy of Richard Hewson, who'd arranged some strings and brass on The Beatles' *Let It Be* album) and some more muscular lead guitar towards the fade.

'Blind Faith' (Egan/Rafferty) (3:21)

Alongside 'What More Could You Want', this is probably the most commercial rocker on the album. A rumbling rhythm guitar with bass and drums joining in make way for a number with definite hints of a Status Quo shuffle, some boogie piano and muffled 'bop-shoo-wop' backing vocals. Gerry sings about how, back in 1964, he and a friend had blind faith in the future. He was 'a young boy, so green', while his friend was older and more experienced. (This was most likely John Byrne, who was seven years older than Gerry, while Joe Egan was two years younger). Blind faith was all they had, 'We just sat around and watched it all go bad'. Had they wanted a third single from the album, they could hardly have done better than this. The Pointer Sisters included a version on their rock covers album *Priority* in 1979 and released it as a single in the US.

'Nothing's Gonna Change My Mind' (Egan) (4:01)

Joe laments the drudgery of a dead-end job with poor money, so it's time to move on and keep travelling: 'Go on living like a rolling stone'. It's another slow, plaintive tune, but given some bite by the country lead guitar about halfway through. Sometimes, Stealers Wheel songs tend to finish all too quickly, but this one takes its time with a lovely fadeout lasting over a minute, allowing their vocal harmonies full rein.

'Steamboat Row' (2:50)

This tune about his father was the first of many songs that Gerry had recorded in his early days and would return to later. The folky simplicity of the Humblebums 1969 recording is retained, though this is about 50 seconds longer, a little slower, and benefits from vocal harmonies and touches of harmonica.

'Back On My Feet Again' (Egan) (2:36)

Joe's song of determination tells of facing a difficult time, having been hiding away, but now he's winning the fight and moving on. It's led by sturdy piano chords and subtle lead guitar, with a feel that brings to mind nothing so much as John Lennon from the Beatles' *White Album* period.

'Who Cares' (3:44)

Gerry had begun work on this number during the *Can I Have My Money Back?* sessions, as evidenced by the two unfinished outtakes previously mentioned. Here's the finished work, just over a minute shorter than its earlier incarnations. The vocal section, taking up almost the first three minutes, hovers around lazily most of the time on a relaxed two-chord pattern on the piano, with the occasional burst of xylophone and a soft shuffling patter on the drums. Lyrically it finds Gerry questioning himself as he's chasing dreams, feeling scared but telling himself he's doing alright even if he's wasting time. The words have undergone a complete change, with none of the 'ever stop to think' or 'friend in Jesus' phrases from the earlier recordings. Just before the three-minute mark, the drums kick into more urgency without altering the tempo, and around 30 seconds of jazz-like saxophone take it to the fade. (On the earlier versions, this coda consisted of partly improvised vocals and lasted around two minutes).

'Everything Will Turn Out Fine' (Re-recording) (Egan/Rafferty) (3:09)
The song itself is discussed more fully above as the band's only item released featuring the temporary six-piece line-up. The album version has a longer (around 20 seconds) and more ambitious intro, using three chords each struck on guitar and piano instead of the eight-second shuffle built mainly around the D chord that opens the single. The break after the second chorus is also very different, with mainly slide guitar that's presumably the work of Jammer or Holland and following the chord sequence used for the verses. As for the song itself, it's in the same key (D), with the same verse/chorus form and more or less the same vocal harmonies.

Ray Jackson of Lindisfarne covered the song as the opening track on his 1980 solo album *In The Night,* produced by Hugh Murphy with Betsy Cook and Gerry on backing vocals and former Stealers Wheel member DeLisle Harper on bass.

Ferguslie Park had two middle-rung hit singles and received positive reviews. In *NME*, Roy Carr opined that the band were 'proving themselves to be superior in every conceivable way to any of their competitors – that's, of course, if they have any!' A&M duly used the quote in their press ads for the album. But it failed to crack the American top 200 album chart despite its popularity with college students and likewise missed the much smaller UK list altogether. The duo's refusal to tour – relying on radio and TV promotion to sell records – was plainly a flawed strategy in a music scene that relied to some extent on artists being seen on stage. A similar fate was to befall another briefly successful British singer-songwriter of the time, Clifford T. Ward, who also preferred to perfect his craft in the studio, eschewing live appearances and interviews. It would lead to a difficult internal situation for Gerry and Joe, with a lack of interest from the record company and management who realised they were failing to deliver after the glory of a transatlantic top-ten single had faded. The album's commercial failure created a level of tension that came close to destroying the partnership.

Right Or Wrong (1975)

Personnel:
Gerry Rafferty: guitar, piano, vocal
Joe Egan: keyboards, guitar, vocal
Bernie Holland, Hugh Burns: guitar
Dave Wintour: bass
Chris Mercer: tenor saxophone
Chris Neill: harp
David Briggs: piano, string arrangements
Geraldine & Josephine: piano, guitar, clavinet
Andy Steele: drums, percussion
Produced by Mentor Williams
Recorded at Apple Studios, London
Record label: A&M
Release date: March 1975
Chart positions: UK: did not chart, US: 201
Running time: 37:51

Soon after the release of *Ferguslie Park,* when Giovanni Dadomo of *Record Mirror* asked the duo why their songs were generally so miserable, Gerry replied that he thought they were actually getting happier. He said the lyrics on the first album reflected what they were going through at the time, notably the problems in getting a band together, auditioning thousands of guitarists and drummers. On the second album, much of the negativity came from their disillusionment with the business side of things. The lyrics on the third hinted that they had gotten their anger at management out of their system, and they seemed to have become more inward-looking.

But when taken as a whole, the mood of most of the songs on all three records is rarely upbeat. The predominant themes are largely a coming to terms with themselves and the world around them and a profound dissatisfaction with the music business. Having obtained a record deal, generous studio time, experienced producers and session musicians, they don't seem deliriously happy with their lot. On his next solo album, Gerry was to write touching songs about his joy as a husband and father. At a time when most songs in the charts were about love and romance, the only number on the first three Stealers Wheel albums that really fitted into the love song category was 'You Put Something Better Inside Me'.

As to why they were dispensing with the services of Leiber and Stoller, Gerry explained that there had been increasing differences in their methods. He said the results of their production had been fine: 'It was just that they wanted to take some things apart and redo them, and we weren't too happy with that idea. We also wanted to take charge of the string arrangements because, quite frankly, we thought their strings were just a bit slushy'.

Moreover, the American partnership's old-school principles didn't make for a relaxed atmosphere. The musicians had to be ready at 2 pm precisely, have a coffee break at exactly 5 pm, and finish at 8 pm on the dot, not going overtime regardless of what they were doing. 'There was a generation gap and a culture gap too. We didn't share a sense of humour or much of anything'.

Despite his initial enthusiasm, Joe had come to realise that they had to part company. The gulf between both partnerships had become too wide, 'plus the fact that they wanted complete control. They're producers from the '50s, and we're artists from the '70s'. Neither side was really happy with the sound of *Ferguslie Park*. Once the third album, *Right Or Wrong,* was ready, Joe told Mike Flood Page of *Sounds* that *Ferguslie Park* 'didn't even have the balls in it that the new album's got, or even the first one for that matter. At least there was more enthusiasm on the first album, no matter how chaotic that was'.

When asked his side of the story some years later, Stoller was more forthcoming about the problems between them: 'I think (Rafferty) viewed us as the enemy. There was something very distasteful to him about us, what we represented to him, crassly commercial, what have you. He was difficult to work with from the get-go'.

Once they'd listened to the songs, the producers knew that with their wealth of experience, they could use some of their own ideas and production tricks to enhance the songs, and they acknowledged that 'In the end, it was a wonderful result'. Nevertheless, they recalled the sessions with mixed feelings. When BBC TV and radio presenter Bob Harris interviewed them on *The Old Grey Whistle Test* not long afterwards, he referred to their work with Stealers Wheel and asked, 'How did that go?' The producers looked at each other and said, 'Pass'.

A&M then recommended that for the next album, they should try Mentor Williams, a songwriter and producer best known for writing Dobie Gray's 'Drift Away'. Gerry and Joe listened to some of Williams' work and were duly impressed. When he came over from America to help make the album, he brought David Briggs, who was to be responsible for string arrangements and, alongside Joe, some of the piano work. Nothing Gerry and Joe said later on gave any reason to suggest it was an inharmonious working relationship. The music was largely the work of a team of four, namely both of them on acoustic guitars and pianos, Dave Wintour on bass, and Andy Steele on drums. One of the additional players was guitarist Hugh Burns, and for him it became part of an excellent association with Gerry, destined to last down the years.

Recording coincided with their final session for John Peel at Radio 1 in April 1975, featuring four songs from the album, with Andy Steele on drums and other session musicians. Peel retained a soft spot for Stealers Wheel and continued to revisit their albums occasionally on his show into the millennium.

While they were recording the album, they were adamant that they would never play any more gigs. Gerry had been completely put off by the idea. He said that when the band was originally formed, there were so many lineup changes, and it just never worked for them. Joe agreed that it had been 'disillusioning'. Their priority was now writing the songs: 'If there's any responsibility at all to the public, it is to make each album better than the one previous'.

Unfortunately for them, the writing and recording of the album would be overshadowed by further business difficulties. The group's management company, Ricochet, had disappeared apparently without a trace, as had the group's royalties. Under the strain of trying to keep Stealers Wheel going after what had been an ill-starred existence, one stroke of bad luck after another, and above all the self-inflicted instability (a running joke in the music papers at the time was whether Rafferty was in the band that week or not), the formerly harmonious partnership between the now manager-less duo was breaking down. Any momentum built by the success of 'Stuck In The Middle' and the two lesser hits had gradually faded away. By the time *Right Or Wrong* and the singles (the title track and 'Found My Way To You') appeared in March and May, respectively, radio stations and the public alike had completely lost interest. The album simply floated out to a total absence of any fanfare, just as its two main creators seemingly went to ground, about to be mired in legal strife that would prevent either from entering a recording studio for some time.

The outer sleeve featured two photographs of them, one a rather hazy image with a background of bare trees. John Byrne's contributions were restricted to a tiny Siamese-twins-like 'Wheelers Steal' rear-view portrait on the front, elaborated on the inner sleeve where they appeared similarly conjoined in the same boiler suit, accompanied by a large hound in the usual whimsical landscape, with variations on their name such as Squealers Meal, Feelers Greel and Dealers Heel.

'Benediction' (Egan/Rafferty) (4:46)

The primary definitions of 'benediction' – a word that appears nowhere in this lyric – are 'Invocation of a blessing' and 'Something that promotes goodness or well-being'. On this – the album's longest track – the words read rather like a series of haphazard thoughts – genuflect (How often do you find that word used in a song?), show respect, papal command, rosary beads, mystical band. It's some comment on mystical icons or church rituals, perhaps. Joe said this was one of three of the album's lyrics that he called really personal, saying they were 'the whole religious thing, and we were brought up in that'. Billy Connolly likewise noted in a TV documentary that he and Gerry were both fascinated by hymns and sometimes sang them while travelling to Humblebums gigs.

This song has one of the duo's loveliest, most beguiling melodies, exquisite vocal harmonies and lush strings with touches of bell chimes, celli, and dreamy guitar courtesy of Hugh Burns, who was to play such a major role in Gerry's music going forward. It may be meaningless or deadly earnest, but it's undeniably poetic and flawlessly executed. The combination of instruments and vocals that take up much of the last two minutes before the fadeout evoke the same mood as some of the more spectacular restrained passages on The Beatles' *Abbey Road*.

'Found My Way To You' (Egan/Rafferty) (3:39)
Stealers Wheel's songs were not generally known for being optimistic, but this one goes totally against the grain. Opening with jaunty piano chords, it's a happy love song from somebody who's found the right partner 'out of the blue'. A distinctive tune, wailing sax, driving drums, strings and inimitable vocal harmonies again combine on one of the album's strongest tracks and a good choice as a second single, even though the duo were already regarded as history where radio stations were concerned.

'This Morning' (Egan/Rafferty) (3:28)
At best, this is a good song and a pleasant idea as far as it goes, but at worst, it's insubstantial and in need of further development. As was so often the case, wonderful folky guitar chords provided the intro, faultless echoing harmony vocals and an attractive tune were about the sum total. The lyric comprised one verse of six fairly short lines, greeting one more morning on the way, daylight opening up the skies, and so on, followed with an instrumental break led by softly picked acoustic, and then three more lines, a bit like a school poem, in fact. Yes, it may be charming, but as it fades out, you're left wondering, 'Is that all?'. The listener's left with a sense that some kind of curve, be it a vocal interlude adding something more dramatic, or else a short instrumental break following an entirely different direction, are on the way. But after repeating the initial pattern, it goes nowhere and just fades out.

'Let Yourself Go' (Egan/Rafferty) (3:27)
As the title suggests, this is more of a rocker, starting with a brisk guitar riff. The lyric suggests memories of teenage dance halls, waiting for everybody to begin, then 'She made me get up right out my seat/Made me get up and move my feet'. Even so, on the whole, it's a little too restrained, and the guitar could've, well, let itself go with more vigour. On the previous two albums, the duo had proven that their folky voices were no impediment to rocking out on occasion. This sounds too inhibited, ironically, in view of the title.

'Home From Home' (Egan/Rafferty) (3:45)
A few soft notes on electric piano introduce more soft-focus lyric ruminations, rather verging on self-pity. Where the home from home may be is a mystery – perhaps two partners being separated by circumstances and desperately needing each other. A prescient hint comes towards the end with 'And when the night-time comes, I try and drink the blues away', and a similar theme was to resurface in the lyrics of Rafferty's later song 'Night Owl'. Delicate

strings, including prominent cello, add sweetness to a sometimes-bitter lyric, with the last minute providing little variation on a three-note phrase that could've been further developed.

'Go As You Please' (Egan/Rafferty) (3:46)
There is more anger here on one of the album's more gritty tracks, directed at memories of schooldays being wrapped in cotton wool and longing to get out, only to find that working at a desk at the local NEB, worrying about his shirt and tie, is every bit as bad. The lead guitar is more upfront, appropriately more fierce, and the drums also add punch.

'Wishbone' (Egan/Rafferty) (3:25)
It's not often that somebody writes a song about killing and cooking a chicken unless it's meant as a metaphor for something else, which, in this case, it seems to be. Here comes the second of the personal numbers, Joe explained, in the form of an indictment against the management in a concealed way. Dark, portentous strings, an insistent electric piano riff and some torrid harmonica all go to show the group could rock with subtlety.

'Don't Get Me Wrong' (3:17)
A relationship has gone wrong – 'You say that I'm a stranger/And you don't know me anymore' – but someone doesn't want to hurt his partner. This – the only solo Gerry song here – has another sad lyric, but it benefits from an Irish flavour with a bustling, almost funky country hoedown on which fiddle and mandolin come to the fore.

'Monday Morning' (Egan/Rafferty) (3:23)
You spend your week slaving away at your desk at the Inland Revenue, but your salvation is going out at the weekend and living it up, getting off on some rock 'n' roll. There's a sharp bluesy intro, with electric piano and guitar powering the song along. Alongside some of the previous songs, this may seem a little lightweight, but it is considerably more fun. According to Joe, it was about a personal experience, but at the same time, it could be about anybody's general situation. 'Everybody has the Monday morning blues'. Again, it sounds too musically subdued in view of the subject matter. Had the group still been playing live at the time, this song would've probably reached its full potential on stage.

'Right Or Wrong' (Egan/Rafferty) (4:55)
This lyric is rather inconsequential and is basically about two strong-willed people out to please themselves, but it benefits from a stronger-than-usual melody and some prominent bass behind the acoustic guitar. Around three minutes in, it changes to a slower tempo and a shuffle rhythm, with improvised vocals, strings soaring ever more extravagantly, and the drummer

working up a good head of steam. The single version fades out earlier and is around 50 seconds shorter.

Although one of the album's better tracks, it lacks the strong hook that would've made it punch with more weight in the marketplace as a single. This was one of several songs that Gerry was to re-record on later albums and probably the only one where the re-recording was a noticeable improvement on the original.

In retrospect, Williams' production was probably not strong enough for the songs. Gerry and Joe were becoming seasoned veterans and were doubtless flexing their muscles to the extent that they were starting to become joint producers of their work, in which case they would've shared in the responsibility. Too much of the album sounds pleasant and well-mannered but simply too lacking in bite – or, to use one of the criticisms they'd made of their earlier work, 'A bit slushy'.

With the release of this third album, Stealers Wheel was effectively past history. In an interview three years later that Gerry gave Michael Gray (at the time his new label's press officer and later his manager), he admitted that the Stealers Wheel period wasn't such a good one for him in terms of what he'd written himself. The best songs they did during that period were his collaborations with Joe: 'On the first album, I feel the best two songs were 'Late Again', which I still think very good, and 'You Put Something Better Inside Of Me'. They're both pretty strong songs. But I wouldn't do them on stage because Joe actually took the lead vocal on both of these'. Gerry opined that the last album of the three was the weakest in terms of the songs and their personal commitment. Having both discovered that their management had gone into liquidation halfway through writing and recording the songs 'didn't exactly produce a great deal of enthusiasm in us for finishing the album'. Perhaps they were too keen to finish what they'd started, get out and simply move on. While Gerry didn't want to be too negative, the whole album had 'pretty bad associations' for him.

There seems to be no critical or fan consensus on which album was the best, with each one having its defenders. If pressed, the present author would choose *Ferguslie Park*, partly because the songs are more consistently strong and because the sound is better, more urgent, more like it's a band playing. This might seem like an odd comment to make in view of the fact that everyone knows it's the work of a duo plus session musicians, but it comes across as a more live performance rather than a collection of songs buffed to a sheen and deprived of some of their bite: a problem that bedevilled some of the cuts on the other two albums.

The largely ignored *Right Or Wrong* was to be followed much later by one more brief flicker of the flame. In 2008, after approaches from iTunes and K-Tel, Tony Williams, Paul Pilnick (switching from guitar to bass) and Rod Coombes made tentative plans to reform the band with close friend Tony

Mitchell. They filmed a video for a re-recording of 'Stuck In The Middle' and were said to be writing new songs. The video, featuring a truncated version of the song, attracted several comments when uploaded to YouTube – some favourable, some not, with one of the latter worded tersely: 'Stealers Wheel, my arse. Rafferty and Egan were the heart of the band'. Presumably as a result of no further interest from the companies concerned, nothing more apart from a press release issued by Henderson Management ('Tribute and party band specialists') was heard of the project.

Gerry and Joe hadn't completely gone their separate ways after dissolving Stealers Wheel, as, at around the same time, they made a rare appearance together as session singers. Producer Ian Samwell asked them to sing backing vocals on the original cast soundtrack of *John, Paul, George, Ringo… And Bert*: Willy Russell's musical based on the story of The Beatles, which premiered in Liverpool in May 1974. The lead vocalist for the songs was Barbara Dickson, who'd been part of the folk music scene in and around Glasgow and had known them for several years. Her delight at working with them was unaffected when they both arrived at the studio, accompanied by clanking noises. It turned out that far from bringing an exotic array of percussion instruments, they were fortified with a plentiful supply of 'carry-oots' and drank them all during the session. But few of their vocal contributions were deemed usable, so Barbara and bass guitarist Pete Zorn had to redo most of them after Gerry and Joe had gone. Readily forgiven, they all remained friends on both sides and later added to each others' work on occasion. Barbara appeared on Gerry's next two solo albums, and he returned the compliment with backing vocals on 'The Times They Are A-Changin'', featured on Dickson's 1994 album of Bob Dylan songs *Don't Think Twice, It's All Right*.

Gerry Rafferty Solo, 1977-2021

While Gerry's desire to continue making music was undimmed, contractual problems were about to bring his career to a temporary halt. A music business that had frustrated him so much left him with a deep distrust of it all. Too much tedious time was spent travelling and engaging in legal issues with Ricochet, which had gone into liquidation. The first year, Gerry told Stuart Wavell, was the worst. He and Joe 'were suing them and they were suing us, and everyone was suing someone to get their hands on the spoils'. Disentangling themselves from the contractual issues took a couple of years. Later, Gerry admitted that the combination of his and Joe's voices was unique, and he was sorry to lose it, which suggests that any difference between them was never personal and was easily smoothed over:

> We never fulfilled our potential, but that was down to the record company and management, not us. We had to stop recording as we were involved in legal wrangles. I'd moved to Glasgow and, for about two years, was making frequent visits to lawyers and accountants in London to sort out the mess.

By early 1977, both could resume their separate careers. Gerry, who was first off the block, returned to Scotland brimming with ideas and busied himself writing more songs on his own, making demos at home on which he sketched out the basic arrangements. These were recorded on a four-track machine at the house of Gerry's wife Carla's parents, with him playing every instrument, including lentil-jar percussion. Soon, he had an album's worth of suitable material to kick-start the next phase.

During this period of hibernation, Gerry was contacted by Jon Brewer, who'd previously been involved in music management, working with clients including David Bowie and Alvin Lee, and had founded his own publishing company, Belfern Music. Having been a fan of Stealers Wheel, Brewer was interested in rescuing Gerry's career and launching him as a solo act, and they met in London to discuss how to proceed. Brewer knew that Gerry had suffered bruising experiences in his career, wouldn't suffer fools or sharks gladly, and might be difficult to please. When they met, Gerry played Brewer a couple of demos for what he envisaged as the next album and asked Brewer if he'd manage him or fund a new album. Brewer agreed to put together not a management agreement but a production agreement to produce three records.

As Gerry was still contracted to A&M but had no intention of recording for the label again, Brewer negotiated a buyout with the label's co-founder Jerry Moss and undertook to find Gerry a new deal elsewhere. According to Brewer's version of events, Anchor and Island Records initially expressed interest, but when Gerry met senior members of both companies in person, any hopes of a deal were quickly dashed. All the songwriter allegedly wanted was to write songs for his daughter. He categorically insisted that he'd do nothing to promote any records he made with them, saying he would not join a band and that he hated everybody in the music industry. Though he was well known for his often uncompromising attitudes towards others, one can be forgiven for thinking this sounded rather too far-fetched to be true. His daughter later commented that Brewer's claims were 'nonsense'. Brewer later said his response to Gerry was to tell him that, at this rate, they would soon run out of record companies.

Next, he arranged a meeting in America with Artie Mogull, President of United Artists Records. Perhaps fortuitously, when they met, Mogull was in a hurry to catch a plane but proved interested enough to agree to a deal without hearing the demos. As a result, Gerry was sufficiently encouraged to contact Hugh Murphy, with whom he'd enjoyed an excellent working relationship while recording *Can I Have My Money Back?*. During the interval of six years or so, Hugh had produced albums by Lindisfarne offshoot Jack The Lad, and Poet Laureate Sir John Betjeman.

The end result was to be Gerry's second solo album, recorded mostly in the summer of 1977, using a formidable lineup of session musicians and singers. It all took place at Chipping Norton Studios, Oxfordshire, a residential facility where everyone involved in the album lived together as a family, worked hard and might spend up to 12 hours on a single song. Only when everyone was happy with their efforts and Gerry agreed that it was the final version did they put down their instruments. Evening meals were always enlivened with the delivery of a barrel of Hook Norton Beer from the brewery. The contrast between such an approach and that of Leiber-Stoller couldn't have been greater.

Sessions were completed towards the end of the year. It never bothered Gerry that his music might not be the flavour of the month in a musical climate where punk was dominating the music-press news pages and the singles chart was dominated by disco: 'Once you start worrying about fashion, there's no point in doing it'. On the album's completion, at a cost of about £18,000, Gerry thought he'd be pleased if it sold over 50,000 copies. Within a few years, it had exceeded 5,000,000 sales.

Having previously worked as half of a duo, then as joint leader of a band, Gerry relished the freedom of being his own master. Now he was working with a collaborator who was not a songwriting partner but a co-producer, whom he could trust and regard as a faithful colleague, rather than somebody telling him what he could and couldn't do. Music came more easily to him than words. He generally listened to traditional folk music at home, and the art of the tunesmith was second nature, as he always had 'a lot of melodies out and about in his head at any given time'. The lyrics required much more effort on his part.

As far back as 1970, when the last Humblebums tracks were being recorded, Gerry said that he'd 'like to get a lot more complex musically on the next album, with songs that last seven or eight minutes', with the proviso that it wouldn't do to bore the listener. It was an ambition or rather an experiment he could never realise with Stealers Wheel. However, when he came to make his first album for United Artists, seven of the ten tracks lasted between five and seven minutes each, or eight if an 11th track, which became a B-side, is included.

Once the album was finished, Gerry's solo career resumed inauspiciously with the release of his first solo single in nearly six years. In September 1977, 'City To City' (edited by about 80 seconds) was released as a single in Britain, Australia and most European countries. At home, it received good reviews, though little TV or radio exposure.

The single was followed by an album of the same name in January 1978. While recording 'Baker Street', Gerry instantly felt that it had 'a touch of magic' and made a strong case for it to be the first single. But he was overruled by United Artists who felt something with a catchy chorus was a safer commercial bet, hence the title song. According to Hugh Murphy in *Billboard*, 'they actually said ('Baker Street') was too good for the public'. Gerry's wish was partly fulfilled when, in the first week of February, the chorus-free song was issued as the follow-up single. Radio exposure followed immediately, with producers and presenters all loving it. Significantly, former Rafferty admirer and now punk-rock guru John Peel excluded Gerry's records from his late-night Radio 1 show, presumably on the grounds that everyone else was giving them adequate exposure. (It might be noted that, according to a Peel website, he still played a Stealers Wheel track five times on his programme between 1987 and 2001, each being an A-side from their debut album.)

In an interview in *The Sun* (Scotland) about ten years later, Gerry said that royalties from 'Baker Street' still made him about £80,000 a year (a figure regularly repeated to this day) and admitted he could live off that alone. In October 2010, the song was officially recognised by BMI (Broadcast Music, Inc.: the US equivalent of the UK Performing Rights Society) as surpassing 5,000,000 plays worldwide. Thanks to the radio, it went to top three in Britain and to number two for six consecutive weeks in America, allegedly denied one week at the summit in July 1978 when the *Billboard* chart compilers were told that Andy Gibb (then at number one with 'Shadow Dancing') was due to appear at an awards ceremony and it might spoil things if 'Baker Street' went to number one that week. It did however achieve such a feat in Canada, Australia and South Africa. Moreover, when *City To City* topped the US album chart for one week that same month, it ended a 24-week stranglehold there by the *Saturday Night Fever* soundtrack.

'Baker Street' was the second of four UK singles from the album. The title track had already come and gone in 1977 without causing a ripple, and during the summer, 'Whatever's Written In Your Heart' (edited to 5:15) and 'Home And Dry' (faded at 3:42) followed likewise without charting. In America, the edited version of 'Right Down The Line' reached number 12 that summer, and 'Home And Dry' reached number 28 early in 1979.

In an interview with Scott Rowley of *Classic Rock*, Brewer said that this US album-chart success happened in the heyday of Payola. Chart positions were based on units shipped and stored in warehouses rather than copies sold over the counter, as long as they were supported by radio airplay. It wasn't illegal; it was the way things worked.

Despite his newly-acquired wealth, Gerry strongly resented Jon's professional *modus vivendi*, his Rolls Royce and his smart offices (the singer would much rather hold meetings in a pub) almost as much as the bruising aspects of showbiz itself. Barbara Dickson (always one of Gerry's greatest admirers and a lifelong friend) readily pointed out that as someone who'd had a very humble upbringing, Gerry enjoyed having money, status and driving nice cars, was proud of his success, but 'Being a pop star is a Faustian pact. You cannot start dictating the terms two years into it'. Dickson also pointed out that Gerry was sometimes criticised for apparent aloofness onstage because he had a cast in his eye that embarrassed him so much that he'd look away from people. He believed that his songs were more important than mere stage presence.

Artist and manager grew further apart, and during a short promotional tour of America, Gerry disregarded Brewer's warning not to do an offered TV interview with David Frost. The exchange didn't prevent *City To City* from going to number one for one week, but Gerry was less than complimentary about the Americans, going on the road, and his fans in general. It was around this time that, in preparation for dates in America, he was greeted on his arrival in New York by a large limousine at the airport, a suite in Central Park and invitations to several parties. (Cue 'Stuck In The Middle' playing in the background, perhaps.) While in New York, Gerry had a panic attack and feared it was a cardiac arrest. Much to the horror of management, the record company and everyone else except the artist himself, all concert dates were promptly cancelled. Others saw it as an extraordinary decision in a career which was at last on a major upswing, and it was to cost him dearly in financial terms.

As Gerry's daughter Martha later put it succinctly, he was simply 'scared by the momentum he was generating and the kind of people his success attracted'. Gerry had just found himself in much the same situation as five years earlier when Stealers Wheel were on the brink of major success and he felt he was losing control. Shortly after the American tour cancellation, he told Ken Emerson of *Rolling Stone* that to be a *star* was the last thing he really wanted. 'What I want is just to develop in terms of my songs, and also to work in other areas'. At various times, he had ideas for projects based on film and musical theatre. None of these came to fruition, but he was already looking beyond to a career based on more than the perpetual treadmill of hit singles, hit albums and sell-out tours.

Meanwhile, the next album was in preparation. Though Brewer had arranged the production agreement that had led to the new record contract, he was not a manager in the usual sense. Aware of the differences between them, he'd doubtless foreseen that their business relationship was unlikely to last long. He told Rowley of *Classic Rock* that before they parted company, Gerry offered to buy himself out of his contract, but this was turned down. Not long afterwards, Capitol Records made an offer that Brewer was reluctant to decline. (Whether this was before or after United Artists ceased operations as a separate label in 1980 is uncertain). Success, he believed, was Gerry's undoing. Gerry 'became someone else, and it was alcohol that took him over'. When Capitol told him they'd offer the singer $5,000,000, he warned the label that it was the worst thing they could do and they would never get another album. He told them that artists write the best songs when they're hungry.

City To City (1978)

Personnel:
Gerry Rafferty: vocals, acoustic guitar, acoustic piano
Tommy Eyre: electric and acoustic piano, organ, synthesizer, brass arrangements
Willy Ray: accordion
Hugh Burns, Jerry Donahue, Nigel Jenkins, Micky Moody, Andy Fairweather Low: guitar
B. J. Cole: steel guitar, dobro
Gary Taylor: bass and backing vocals
Henry Spinetti: drums
Graham Preskett: fiddle, mandolin, ARP string synthesizer, string and brass arrangements
Glen LeFleur: percussion, drums
Hugh Murphy: tambourine
Raphael Ravenscroft: saxophone
Paul Jones: harmonica
Rab Noakes, Roger Brown, Barbara Dickson, Vivienne McAuliffe, John McBurnie, Joanna Carlin: backing vocals
Produced by Hugh Murphy and Gerry Rafferty
Recorded at Chipping Norton Studios, Oxfordshire
Record label: United Artists
Release date: January 1978
Charts: UK: 6, US: 1, GER: 3, AUS: 3, NE: 5, NZ: 6, Au: 9, SWE: 9
Running time (original release): 51:11; (2011 remaster, bonus tracks): 85:20

According to Gerry's daughter Martha, the songs on this album 'had been hibernating' for a long time as basic ideas that he gradually completed in the home studio where he spent time every day. As a child of about six, she became familiar with the basic tracks that he used to play on the car stereo when they were driving around Glasgow, and she 'always had a sense that there was a touch of magic in those songs'. The result was an album of ten numbers that had been gestating for a while and Gerry had been longing to complete. They just flowed once the legal barriers to further work in the recording studio had been lifted.

John Byrne provided not one but two sleeve designs for the record. The first was a stark one of a young punk with a nose rather the worse for wear after a fight and a snakeskin jacket with a Gerry Rafferty badge. United Artists turned it down and requested a more user-friendly alternative. John admitted that his second attempt, which showed Gerry with a solid-body electric guitar over his knee against a dark urban sky, was much better.

'The Ark' (5:40)
The melody for this song had been in Gerry's musical in-tray since he recorded *Can I Have My Money Back?* and he tried to finish it then but could

never write a bridge that really satisfied him. It proved to be difficult, but he liked the basic idea so much ('The best melodies stay with me anyway, I don't need to write them down') that he was determined to complete it for the second solo album. It reflects the influence that traditional music had always had on him, and it's the closest the album gets to pure folk. Australian bush band, The Bushwackers, play the introductory Celtic-flavoured passage on fiddle, concertina and bodhran, one of the members being Paisley-born Louis McManus Jnr., while Graham Preskett added fiddle and mandolin.

The lyric refers to darkness falling as we're invited to trust the guiding light, join the journey and 'find a ship to take us on the way'. It was inspired by a book Gerry had read on the significance of the ark in literal and symbolic terms and by a theory on the story of the flood – namely that the ark was a knowledge or a faith, a teaching that came to the fore whenever a civilisation was threatened.

'Baker Street' (6:05)

The largely autobiographical song for which Gerry will always be remembered and which began its life as a series of handwritten lines on a sheet of paper headed 'Baker St. Blues' was one of the last that he completed for the album. Part of the inspiration came from his friendship with session guitarist and one-time Stealers Wheel member Iain Campbell, the guy 'with that look on his face', a real-life 'rolling stone' who wanted to settle down, give up the booze and the one-night stands. In the summer of 1977, Gerry visited Campbell, who was living in a mews house just off London's Baker Street. For a while, they sat around 'playing guitars until the sun came up'. Gerry regularly took the train between Glasgow and Euston, and one day as he walked to the station with guitar case in hand, it seemed 'Such a beautiful morning, such a positive feeling'. He began writing the song on the train ride north and finished it a few days later at home in Scotland. Some lines referred directly to Campbell; others were based on Gerry's own personal reflections. He said the song was about 'the loneliness and alienation of being a stranger in a big city when I wanted to be home with my wife and child'. Years later, that child would say that in the song could be heard 'the soaring, transcendent optimism of the promise of a new life; the discovery that life could indeed be ultimately meaningful'.

The opening lines are sombre. An initial draft reveals that it underwent some changes. In verse one, the narrator is winding his way down the street, light in his head and dead on his feet. The next lines were:

Oh brother what a day
You wanna hide yourself away and forget about everything

Look up to see if there's a light in her place
She opens the door with that look on her face

Above: Gerry Rafferty on stage as part of the six-piece Stealers Wheel at Pinkpop Festival, Geleen, Netherlands, in June 1973. (*Alamy*)

Left & below: *The Humblebums* (1969), or *The New Humblebums* according to label and rear sleeve, marked Gerry's and Billy's debut on vinyl and was the first of several distinctive sleeves designed by John Patrick Byrne. (*Transatlantic/ Sanctuary Ltd/BMG Rights Management*)

Left: *Open Up The Door* (1970) was released as the duo were going their separate ways. (*Transatlantic/Sanctuary Ltd/ BMG Rights Management*)

Right: The Humblebums had opened up the door away from the folk clubs to vastly more successful careers on their own. (*Transatlantic/Sanctuary Ltd/ BMG Rights Management*)

Left: *Can I Have My Money Back* (1971) was regarded by some as the first Stealers Wheel album in all but name. (*Transatlantic/Sanctuary Ltd/ BMG Rights Management*)

Right: *Stealers Wheel* (1972), the group's eponymous debut, spawned the transatlantic top-ten single 'Stuck In The Middle'. (*A&M/Universal Music Enterprises*)

Left: Gerry Rafferty and Billy Connolly in the studio, c.1969. (*Mike Hale*)

Below: Billy and Gerry, their attention momentarily distracted as they unwind with a pint or two in 1969. (*Mike Hale*)

Right: Gerry around the time of the formation of Stealers Wheel, 1971. (*Transatlantic/ Sanctuary Ltd/BMG Rights Management*)

Below: Gerry at the piano. He always had a cache of original tunes to which he would write lyrics afterwards. (*Universal Enterprises*)

Above: The original Stealers Wheel – Rab Noakes, Gerry, Roger Brown – in 1971, though Rab and Roger left before the first album was recorded. (*Davidson Rockpix*)

Below: Stealers Wheel – Paul Pilnick, DeLisle Harper, Rod Coombes, Luther Grosvenor, Gerry, with Joe Egan in front – in 1973. All but Gerry and Joe left shortly afterwards. (*Davidson Rockpix*)

Above: Joe Egan on German TV's *Beat Club*, 1974.

Right: Gerry and producer Hugh Murphy in the studio, 1977. (*Mike Hale*)

Left: The design of *Ferguslie Park* (1973) suggested that Gerry and Joe might be contemplating an alternative career in dairy farming. (*A&M/Universal Music Enterprises*)

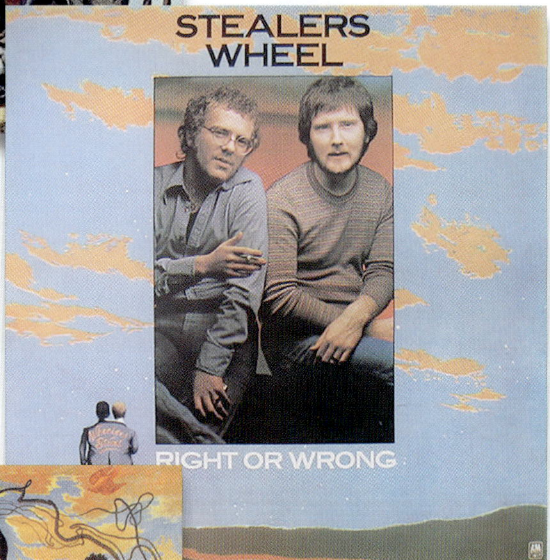

Right & below: Outer (right) and inner (below) sleeve designs of the final album, *Right Or Wrong* (1975), which was completed under difficult circumstances and released to complete indifference. (*A&M/Universal Music Enterprises*)

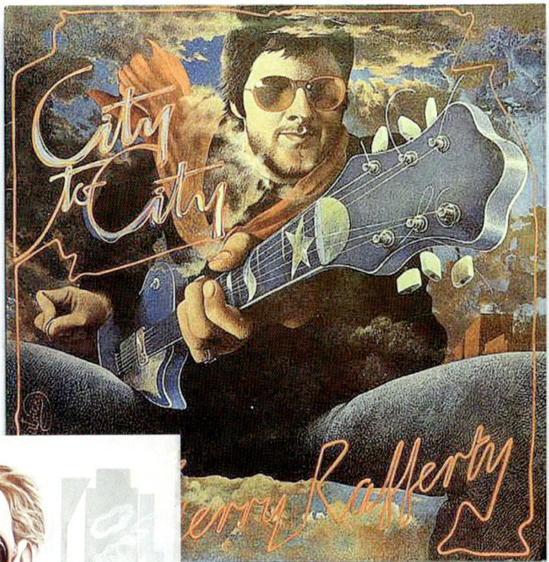

Right: *City To City* (1978) was Gerry's second and most successful solo album by far, with sales reaching 5,000,000 within a few years. (*United Artists/Universal Music*)

Left: John Byrne's initial design for *City To City*. We can guess why it was rejected. (*United Artists/Universal Music*)

Right: *Night Owl* (1979) was Gerry's only album to feature two UK top-30 hits: the title track and 'Get It Right Next Time'. (*United Artists/Universal Music*)

Left: The sheet music to 'Night Owl', a track which revealed a painfully honest lyric about how he coped with his new-found success. (*United Artists/Universal Music*)

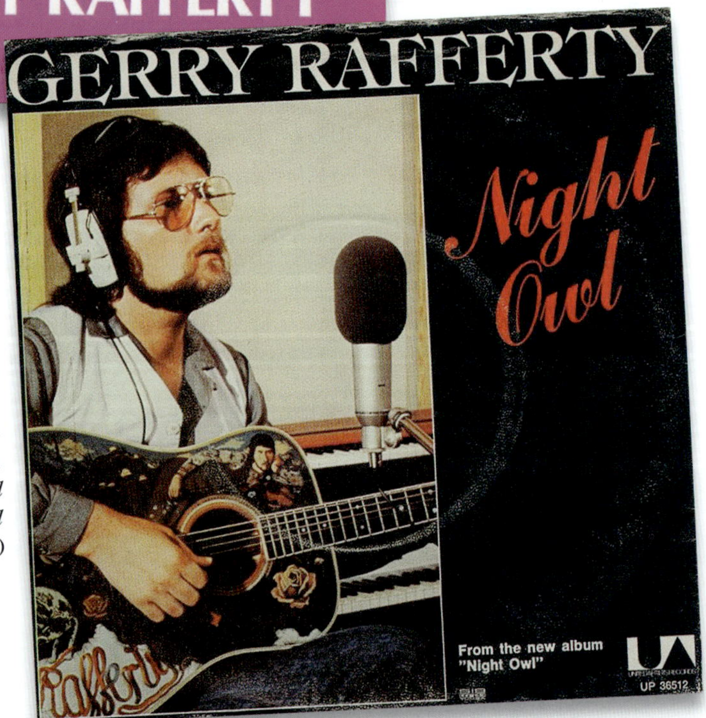

Right: This Swedish picture sleeve of 'Night Owl' showing Gerry playing the acoustic guitar was painted by John Byrne. (*United Artists/Universal Music*)

Right: An American music press advert for *Night Owl* and the top-30 hit 'Days Gone Down', which was not released as a single in the UK. (*United Artists/Universal Music*)

Below: A British music press advert for 'Bring It All Home', including UK tour dates for March and April 1980. (*United Artists/Universal Music*)

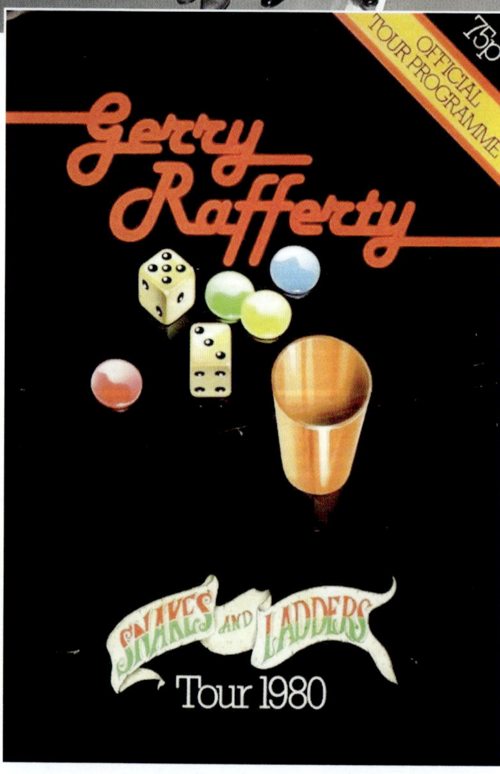

Above: Gerry at The British Rock and Pop Awards 1978 presentation ceremony with members of ELO and The Barron Knights, plus Robin Gibb, Ian Dury, Nick Lowe and Leo Sayer, April 1979. (*Mike Hale*)

Left: A programme for the 1980 *Snakes And Ladders* tour, with Richard and Linda Thompson as support.

Right: *Snakes And Ladders* (1980) failed to emulate the success of the two previous albums. (*United Artists/ Universal Music*)

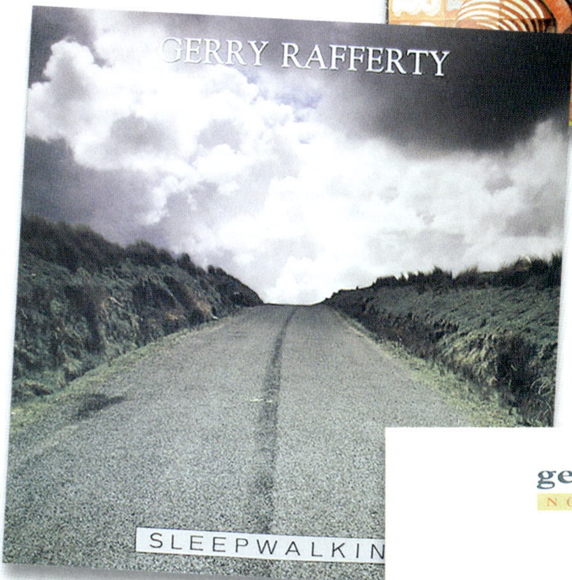

Left: *Sleepwalking* (1982) found Gerry working with a new producer, embracing 1980s synthesiser sounds, and for the first time in years, eschewing a John Byrne sleeve design. (*Liberty/Universal Music*)

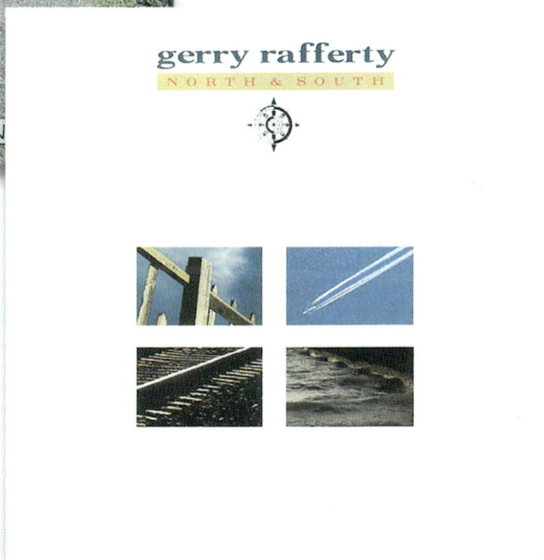

Right: *North And South* (1988) dwelt on Gerry's reflections as a Scotsman needing to stay in touch with his roots while living in and around London. (*London/Universal Music*)

Left: The German picture sleeve of 'Moonlight And Gold', a single from *North And South*. Germany was always one of Gerry's most successful overseas markets. (*London/Universal Music*)

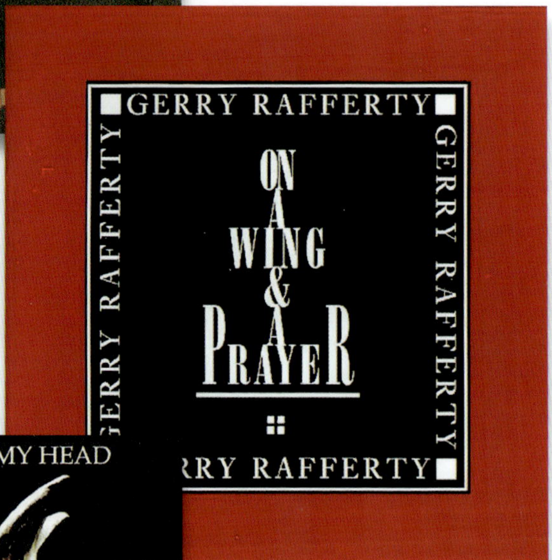

Right: *A Wing And A Prayer* (1992), several songs on which were inspired by the end of his marriage. Joe Egan appears on eight of the 12 tracks. (*A&M/ Polydor/Universal Music*)

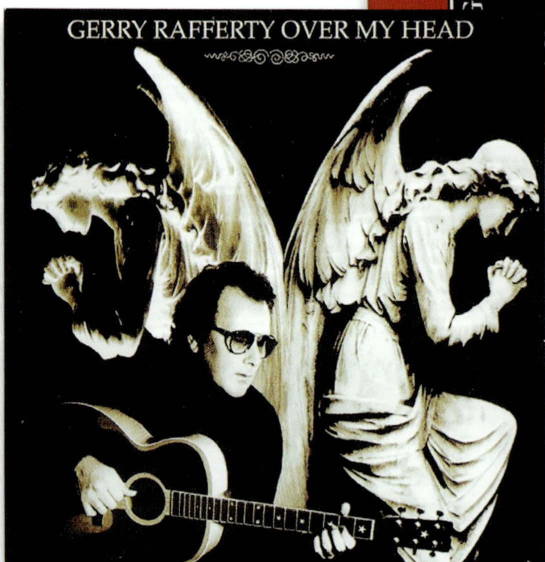

Left: *Over My Head* (1994), the final album produced by Hugh Murphy, suffered from poor promotion and failed to chart anywhere. (*Polydor/Universal Music*)

Right: *Another World* (2000) was initially released in download form and on CD in 2003 with a slightly altered track listing. (*Hypertension*)

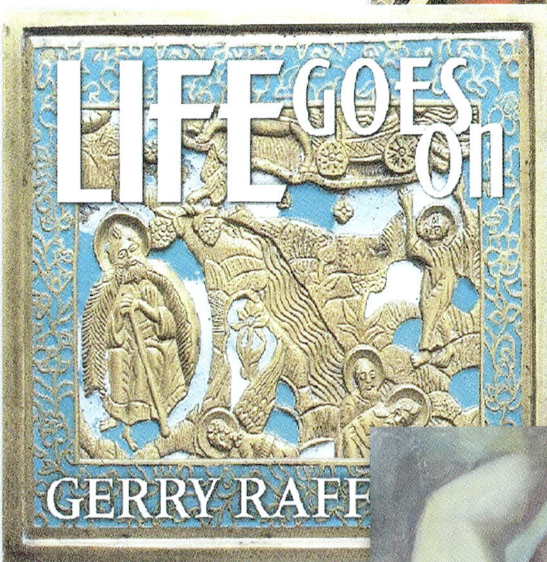

Left: *Life Goes On* (2009) featured several new edits of previous recordings, Christmas carols and a cover version of a Beatles song. (*Hypertension*)

Right: *Rest In Blue* (2021), the posthumous release overseen and co-produced by Gerry's daughter Martha, with contributions from musicians who had worked with him over the years. (*Parlophone/ Universal Music*)

Left: Gerry, around 1992, shortly before his final brief tour of Britain and Europe. (*Hawkhead PA*)

Below: Gerry, about 2000, at the time he recorded *Another World*. (*Hawkhead PA*)

And you wonder why you came
You know it's gonna be the same

It subsequently became 'another crazy day' followed by a visit to the pub to drink the night away and forget about everything. He needs to, as he's in a city that has so many people but no soul, one that he naïvely used to think 'held everything', but now he finds out he's wrong. One day, he'll be happy, but he's crying now.

Lonely and in need of friendly company, it's not a mystery lady he visits (as it was in the draft), but an old pal with whom he spends the evening chatting, maybe even strumming a guitar. This is Iain Campbell, the happy drifter who has a dream of buying himself some land, going onto the wagon and giving up those one-night stands. But Ian's a rolling stone and is never going to stop moving. Finally, there's optimism at the end of the song as the narrator wakes to a sunny new morning, and at last, he's going home. In his case, 'home' means going back to Scotland to his wife and daughter and also going back to his recording career, with all the business obstacles behind him. All's well that ends well.

Years later, Martha remarked that the song was partly inspired by and was, in fact, a lyrical version of Colin Wilson's 1956 book *The Outsider*. Gerry was reading the book while working on the album. Wilson's book was about the psychology of the outsider writer.

The song's arrangement is unusual in that it has not one intro but two – the first with lush, almost ambient, other-worldly chords underpinned by subtle percussion. At 0:23, it morphs with the aid of a simplified drum tattoo into the familiar sax intro that continues for 45 seconds. That sax phrase reappears after the first two verses at 2:05, after verses three and four at 3:47, with the first intro reappearing at 4:22, followed by the 'seagull' lead guitar break at 4:48, and the sax returning from 5:22 to fade. The single edit, lasting 4.07, omits the repeated intro and brings the guitar break in at the end of the second verse, with a brief reprise of 15 seconds for the sax until the fade. An added twist is provided by not only the skilful pattern of minor chords but also a subtle change in key with the sax riff in D switching swiftly to verses in A.

Gerry originally wanted the sax phrase to be played on electric guitar or piano, which he and Hugh tried, then with voices instead, until they decided that neither worked. Gerry wanted 'a lonely, big-city sound'. Hugh was listening to a Joni Mitchell record, and there was a sax playing and it really sounded great, so he realised that a sax would provide the street sound they were after. He initially wanted Pete Zorn to play it, but he was unavailable as 'his lip had gone'. When Raphael Ravenscroft was recommended, Gerry said, 'With a name like that, I reckoned he had to be good, and he was'. Raph arrived 'with this real beat-up old saxophone. It was falling apart with the keys falling off and gaffer tape everywhere', but he played the part to perfection.

There have been questions about the origins of what became one of the most iconic sax phrases in popular music history. Raph said that most of what he played was an old blues riff, and he was never handed a piece of music to perform, but the song 'had several gaps in it when he was hired to play, and he filled them'. Not long afterwards, Brewer had a visit from the persistent Raph, who considered his contribution to 'Baker Street' substantial enough to warrant a joint songwriting credit or a percentage of publishing money. For once, Brewer and Rafferty were of like mind. A session musician employed to play a few bars of music that had already been written and demoed for the song was entitled to his fee and no more. A demo of the song which appeared on a 2011 remastered reissue, confirmed that Gerry had already written an arrangement for the melody that became the sax part, initially played on guitar. As the story goes, when Raph's request was refused, he lost his temper and told Brewer he was going to steal something from him. A few days later, Brewer's personal assistant vanished. He later heard that she had married the saxophonist. (This might sound a little like comic drama, but for the record, Raph had three marriages, two divorces, and separated from his last wife.)

In 2011, he complained that his part was out of tune and was gutted when he heard it played back. He never had a chance to re-record his contribution, as he wasn't involved when the song was mixed. 'I'm irritated because it's out of tune. Yeah, it's flat, by enough of a degree that it irritates me at best'. No less tiresome was the often-circulated story, which he once confirmed and later denied, that he was paid a session fee of £27, the cheque bounced, and so it was framed and hung on his solicitor's wall. Had this been true, Raph probably wouldn't have been too keen to play on two of Gerry's subsequent albums or be part of the band on two tours, which he was. Finally, another old chestnut was that TV host Bob Holness played the sax riff, an idea that's said to have been either Ravenscroft's own joke or a quip by journalist and presenter Stuart Maconie in *NME*. When it was mentioned to Holness, he said the solo was tremendous and he wished he *had* played it, but no, he couldn't play a note.

That leaves one or two more twists in this protracted saga. Did Gerry really write that hook in the first place? In 1968, American saxophonist Steve Marcus released the jazz-rock fusion album *Tomorrow Never Knows*. Alongside cover versions of various tunes, including the Beatles title track, was the piece 'Half A Heart', which was apparently written for him by close friend and vibraphonist/composer Gary Burton. Marcus died in 2005, but a few years later, journalist Adam Chandler contacted Burton to ask if he was aware of the connection. After reading about 'Baker Street', which he'd never heard (except possibly on the radio), and listening to the two pieces of music recorded ten years apart, he said the notes and phrasing were so similar that Ravenscroft *must've* heard 'Half A Heart'. That seemed to surprise Burton less than the fact that the internet and the original Steve Marcus album had credited Burton with composing the number. He said he had no recollection of writing it.

Leaving this diversion on one side, Gerry was astonished by what the song achieved. In 1988, he told Colin Irwin, 'I suppose it's become one of those songs like 'A Whiter Shade Of Pale' or something that people always remember. I'm duly flattered. I'm pleased I was able to produce something like that, something so successful because it was a good piece of work'. 'Baker Street' was arguably the 1970s equivalent of 'A Whiter Shade Of Pale', in that it was an epic, groundbreaking single would be very hard to follow up, in the eyes of the public at least, and would ultimately overshadow everything he recorded later.

Ravenscroft was not the only 24-carat musician on the record. It also owed much to the guitar work of Hugh Burns, who'd been working with veteran bassist Jack Bruce when he received a call to come and play on the album. It was probably no surprise, as he'd already played on *Right Or Wrong*. Nevertheless, he always regarded it as 'great good fortune' that he was able to contribute so much to Gerry's recorded work: 'I probably did more music with him than any other musician'. Even though they both realised at once that guitar wouldn't be right for the phrase that was to be immortalised on sax, *City To City* marked the start of a long and harmonious musical relationship between both men.

For Burns, 'Baker Street' had many qualities that made it so unique: 'The lyric and the melody fuse beautifully, and the lyric is complemented by the melody. The music itself – the orchestration, so to speak – complements the lyric in a perfect way'. In the song's unorthodox nature and structure, Hugh considered it comparable to Queen's 'Bohemian Rhapsody': 'It's not just opening/verse/chorus. It doesn't do that. It goes through a little kind of journey, it takes you through a journey, and so, in some sense, it's a very complete composition, which is unusual for popular music at that time. People weren't quite used to that'. He likewise dismissed the theory that the sax riff had been taken from any other piece of music, explaining that there were only 12 chromatic notes and there are many instances where phrases are very similar.

In the UK, a remix of the single returned it to the top 75 for four weeks in 1990, peaking at number 53. After Gerry's death in January 2011, it re-charted for one week at number 55 on downloads alone.

Several other artists have released their versions of the song, including Undercover, who took it to number two in the UK in 1992, Waylon Jennings, Ann Wilson of Heart, and Foo Fighters. The sax break was featured in an episode of the cartoon series *The Simpsons* 'played by Lisa Simpson'. Gerry loathed the Undercover version, calling it 'dreadful, totally banal – it's a sad sign of the times'. Nevertheless, it sold about 3,000,000 in Europe and America, earning an estimated £1.5,000,000. As a result, Gerry could afford to turn down regular offers to use the song for advertising. The Foo Fighters 1997 version – a B-side on their 'My Hero' single, subsequently added to the 10th-anniversary reissue of their album *The Colour And The Shape* – offered a more-adventurous treatment, with some light and shade in restraint, bombast on alternate verses, and substituted guitars for sax (as well as 'crack' for 'booze' in the second half). Slash said that his guitar solo towards the end of Guns N' Roses' 'Sweet Child O' Mine' had been inspired by the solo in 'Baker Street', though he didn't indicate whether it was the sax break or guitar solo.

'Right Down The Line' (4:28)

Next to 'Baker Street', this is often hailed as one of the finest songs of Gerry's solo career. It's a simple, unvarnished love song written and delivered straight from the heart. It was for his wife Carla, who'd always supported and believed in him since his days as an aspiring musician and stood by him 'through some really heavy times', and it was just his way of saying thanks. A crystal clear steel guitar intro and later break from B. J. Cole, tasteful, delicate organ behind the verses with added piano on the bridge from Tommy Eyre, and unobtrusive bass and drums make this four minutes-plus a model of musical restraint at its best. Lines like '...as constant as a northern star/The brightest light that shines' evoke pure romance without excessive sentimentality.

The second of three singles in America, it peaked at number 12, reaching 33 in New Zealand and 93 in Australia, despite tanking completely as the fourth single in Britain. In 2012, Bonnie Raitt recorded a reggae version for her album *Slipstream*.

'City To City' (5:02)

A fourth top-drawer song in a row, and totally different from the preceding three – that really is the mark of a quality album. The title track was the first recorded and was the first British single, taking its bow in September 1977 as a taster for what was to follow. For Gerry it had been an easy create as he'd long 'wanted to write a good train song', with regular journeys between Glasgow and London giving him the inspiration. Bluegrass fiddle and a couple of train impersonations serve as the intro for what must be the most irresistibly catchy of the ten tracks.

The chorus that hits home straight away, the optimistic message 'Goodnight train is gonna carry me home', excellent country fiddle, steel guitar, and above all, Paul Jones' superlative harmonica work combine in a song that's shining just as bright as the moon 'and a light made of silver' coming through the window in the third verse. With an interesting nod to earlier days, Rab Noakes and Roger Brown are among the backing voices on the chorus, and it sounds like they're all having fun. Hugh plays tambourine, so for the first time, he can be heard on record. While Barbara Dickson doesn't sing on this track, she does elsewhere on the album. She recorded her own version of this song as a single from her 1978 album *Sweet Oasis*.

'Stealin' Time' (5:58)

For the end of side one of the original vinyl, the lyric of this simple, exquisite ballad celebrates in a relaxed fashion the joy of just sitting and watching the sky, letting the day roll by. 'Forget about everything': Gerry evidently liked that phrase. The soft, crystal-clear electric piano is reinforced by more steel guitar, with only the gentlest occasional drumming.

'Mattie's Rag' (3:25)
Having recorded songs for his wife and parents on earlier albums, Gerry now wrote one for his daughter, and it's easily the shortest song on the album. Not having seen Mattie (Martha) for a long time, he's been away a long time and can't wait until he gets home and she opens the door. To celebrate, he's come back with a big surprise for her: an old mandolin man who will sing for her if she winds him up. Well, she has a real one, too, the one that's just arrived back. After a fade-in intro, the full band is in-tow, with strings and brass, B. J. Cole playing a dobro solo, and clarinet playing over the last minute. As the title subtly hints, it's almost ragtime in feel.

'Whatever's Written In Your Heart' (6:37)
In terms of musical accompaniment, this is the starkest song on offer, and the longest. Some view this song as probably the most heartfelt Gerry ever wrote. Emotionally, it's a powerful piece, but a very brave choice for a single, which it was, if only in Britain (with the B-side of 'The Ark' in Germany), edited by just over a minute. Hot on the heels of a top-three hit, it sank without a trace.

The only instruments are Tommy Eyre's piano and Moog (the former reminiscent of early Elton John), with Gerry, Barbara Dickson and Joanna Carlin (who later reverted to her real name of Melanie Harrold on two of Gerry's later albums) on backing vocals. It's a sad, gospel-like epitaph to a love that has failed, as one partner realises he's never been able to communicate properly with the other. He came to talk in an effort to put things right, thinking he might get through: 'I heard her speak/But all the words were dead/We talked all night and left it all unsaid'.

Despite its lack of chart success, it remained a favourite of Gerry and the family, who performed it at his funeral. He was particularly proud that he wrote much of it in one night, adding lyrics and verses to a chorus he'd had for a while, and recording it the next day. He later modestly called it 'probably one of the better tracks on the album'.

'Home And Dry' (4:56)
Evidently the airborne equivalent of the title track, Gerry is back on his travels in this one, flying in a 'silver bird' across the skies. He's on his way home, presumably to be reunited with his family: 'Just one more hour and I'll be home and dry'. It's a mid-tempo track, with synth the prominent instrument behind his vocals much of the time and a soaring guitar refrain to bring the song to fade. The third American single, it reached number 28 early in 1979.

'Island' (5:15)
A relaxed, slow, almost Caribbean atmosphere pervades this summery song. Raph's sax intro begins proceedings and continues throughout much of the number, supplemented with touches of steel guitar, accordion and organ, adding hints of a jazz feel punctuated by soft vocals. While the word 'island' appears nowhere, there are hints of the two main characters having shared a city life during which they were strangers for so long; they had dreams together that crumbled one by one, and now they're making a new start in a paradise with blue sky and sunshine, where they can 'Walk outside and let the breeze blow all our cares away'.

'Waiting For The Day' (5:45)
The album's final song has more references to travel – counting the lights on the motorway and night coming down as a warm wind blows through the trees. This time he's wishing he was with his loved one or his family so far away, hence 'waiting for the day'. Another ominous line states bluntly, 'Sleep won't come, I need a drink'. Alongside the title track, it's the most uptempo track here, with a bustling rhythm driven by piano from both Tommy and Gerry. About halfway through, there's a bridge during which nearly all the instruments disappear behind the vocal, only to return to top gear for the next verse, which is followed by Hugh's impassioned guitar break. The bridge returns afterwards, with a final verse and a reprise of Hugh's guitar solo as it fades out.

Bonus Tracks 2011 (Double CD, remastered, Parlophone)
'Big Change In The Weather' (5:23)
The track that started life as the B-side to 'Baker Street' is a comparatively brisk, almost funky piece of work with an energetic rhythm provided mostly by guitar and congas, the last two minutes being taken up with Hugh's guitar solo that comes close to screaming in its wildest moments. It's so fast that one suspects the recording might have been slightly sped up. The lyric reads as an open letter to someone Gerry knew long ago, when they used to be together before he had long hair and when he used to bare his soul to him. Later, he became a hero, with people lining up to feed his ego. 'If your head is in a mess/Why don't you give your mouth a rest?'. Was it directed at his fellow former Humblebum? There are similarities to John Lennon's notorious 'How Do You Sleep?' on *Imagine,* or going back further, Bob Dylan's 'Positively 4th Street' comes to mind.

In May 1979, Colin Irwin of *Melody Maker* raised the issue of 'bad blood with Billy Connolly at one time'. Gerry told him that their split had been perfectly amicable and that both of them later made a couple of unfortunate remarks to the music press. 'Nothing to worry about. We've met subsequently and it's fine'. A few feathers had been ruffled on both sides, but the old friendship was rekindled and lasted until the very end.

'Instrumental Intro' (0:38)
An ethereal-sounding phrase made up of synths and guitars, sounding loosely like the germ of the later *Night Owl* track 'Take The Money And Run'.

'Big Change In The Weather' (Demo) (4:09)
The demo is just over a minute shorter than the finished item, with a very short guitar break at the end. It's rather less fired-up and is mainly acoustic, with a drum unit and *bossa nova* sidestick, with acoustic guitar played throughout and a guitar break adding fills over the top.

'Baker Street' (Demo) (5:23)
This was the renowned demo which demonstrated beyond all doubt that Raph didn't compose the sax riff himself, but that Gerry had worked it out note-for-note in advance and sketched it on guitar. The first 20 seconds are waves of ambient sound that wash over the listener, punctuated by softly billowing cymbal crashes at strategic intervals. More than a minute longer than the single edit and about 50 seconds shorter than the album version, it includes an approximation of the intro, though it repeats the guitar motif that would be played on sax several times, but without any prototype for Hugh Burns' solo.

'Mattie's Rag' (Demo) (3:02)
This is largely a Gerry solo track on acoustic guitar, with a few wordless vocals before the end. There is some basic percussion to keep time, plus what sounds like a rudimentary guitar to fill in little gaps here and there.

'Take The Money And Run' (Early studio version) (5:16)
As the words 'studio version' imply, this is more than a demo, with its powerful synth work, lead guitar and drums, indicating a track that was already close to completion before being put aside to be reworked for the next album.

'Stealin' Time' (Demo) (4:31)
This is Gerry on acoustic guitar with a little help from tambourine and another guitar part overdubbed at the end as an idea for a solo.

'City To City' (Demo) (5:16)
A little slower than the finished version, this run-through features Gerry on acoustic guitar, with lead guitar at appropriate intervals.

'Instrumental Outro' (0:31)
A reprise of the intro that ended up as 'Take The Money And Run'.

When the record flew out of the shops worldwide, Gerry found the general reaction and subsequent sales difficult to believe. It was the first time that success in the album charts had come his way, and it came with a resounding bang:

> I would've been quite happy if the album had sold a respectable figure, like 500,000 worldwide. I thought I'd have been doing pretty well. You just write the best songs you can, do your best and see what happens. I thought the songs were good, but I didn't expect this.

Between 1 and 14 June, Gerry and a six-piece band hit the road on the City To City tour of 12 dates, including venues in Coventry, Derby, Croydon, Birmingham, Newcastle and Bristol, with Rab Noakes to open for them. Dire Straits were due to support them as special guests at Edinburgh Odeon for one show and possibly one or two others, but in the music papers, Rab had been announced as being on the bill for every concert. Mark Knopfler's band, who themselves were on the verge of breaking big, were beginning their own headlining tour around the same time, and it was clearly in their interests to go out on the road independently as the main attraction as much as possible.

Unlike the sub-standard gigs that Gerry had played with Stealers Wheel, he was fully in control this time and the band were rehearsed to perfection. The most prestigious was a show at the Theatre Royal, Drury Lane, on 11 June, where he and his team (Julian Littman on guitar, mandolin and piano; Gary Taylor on bass; Liam Genockey on drums; Tommy Eyre and Jeff Bannister on keyboards, and naturally Raph on saxes and flute) put on a rapturously-received performance. According to a review by Tony Bacon in *Sound International*, the set began with 'The Ark' and 'Stuck In The Middle' and included songs from the Humblebums era and the first solo album. Inevitably, the bulk of the set was given over to the current album, as they delivered track after track with 'the ease of a practised conjurer producing rabbit after rabbit'. 'Baker Street', he opined, turned out to be 'an even greater *tour de force* in the flesh than on record', with some instrument swapping in the keyboard department, including Littman 'doing a stint on grand for the verses, rushing out front for his cataclysmic explosion of a guitar solo'. The show ended with an encore of 'Stand By Me'.

After the tour, Gerry and Hugh Murphy returned to Chipping Norton Studios to make album number three, *Night Owl*. Several of the musicians and singers who'd played on the previous one came with them, among them Hugh Burns, Raphael Ravenscroft, Tommy Eyre and Graham Preskett. To these were added veteran session keyboard player Pete Wingfield, former Steeleye Span accordion player John Kirkpatrick, ex-Fairport Convention guitarist Richard Thompson and his wife Linda, and drummer Liam Genockey, who'd played on the previous summer's live dates and was to be a recurring presence on future albums.

City To City had set the bar high, becoming one of the major music success stories of 1978, yet its follow-up, *Night Owl,* was even better. It spawned hit singles on both sides of the Atlantic, even if sales and chart positions were less spectacular than they'd been a year earlier.

By this time, Gerry had settled into a comfortable working relationship with his producer. Hugh provided him with invaluable support whenever needed, even to the extent of accompanying him to the recording of a Dutch TV show where he needed somebody to mime Paul Jones' harmonica playing on 'City To City'. This matter of miming for such promotional appearances was becoming anathema to Gerry, and before long, he flatly refused to do them altogether. Betsy Cook – one of his regular backing vocalists and later occasional keyboard player on his albums (and also the future Mrs. Hugh Murphy) – said that Gerry always had a broad vision for the songs, and Hugh was the person who 'put them into the landscape'. Fellow backing vocalist Linda Thompson – who similarly had the greatest admiration for Gerry as a person and artist – said that Hugh was the only person who could really put up with Gerry's perfectionism and sometimes uncertain temper for any length of time because he was always so calm.

In April 1979, The British Rock & Pop Awards ceremony was hosted by David Jensen at the Café Royal, London, to celebrate the music of the preceding year. Gerry was presented with an award for 'Baker Street' as the best single of 1978 and looked distinctly ill at ease after Jensen presented him with his trophy and he posed for the cameras with fellow winners, including Robin Gibb, Leo Sayer, Ian Dury and Nick Lowe, members of ELO and The Barron Knights. It was the first and last time Gerry was ever seen at such an occasion. The cult of celebrity was the very last thing he wanted. Years later, he told Martha that he really valued being the observer. Martha said 'Once you become too famous, you become the observed, which for him was a definition of hell really, not to be able to walk around freely'. As Mark Knopfler once said, 'Success is great, but fame is what comes out of the exhaust pipe of a car. It's something you don't really want'.

Night Owl (1979)

Personnel:
Gerry Rafferty: vocals, acoustic piano, Polymoog, acoustic guitar, string arrangements
Graham Preskett: acoustic and electric piano, string synthesizer, keyboards, fiddle, mandolin, string arrangements and conductor
Pete Wingfield: organ
Tommy Eyre: acoustic and electric piano, synthesizer
John Kirkpatrick: accordion
Richard Brunton: electric guitar, lap steel
Hugh Burns: guitar
Richard Thompson: mandolin, guitar
Mo Foster, Gary Taylor: bass
Liam Genockey: drums
Frank Ricotti: percussion
Raphael Ravenscroft: lyricon, saxophone
Richard Harvey: pennywhistle, pipe organ, recorder, synthesizer
Gavyn Wright: string leader
Betsy Cook, Barbara Dickson, Linda Thompson: backing vocals
Produced and engineered by Gerry Rafferty and Bill Murphy
Recorded at Chipping Norton Studios, Oxfordshire
Record label: United Artists
Release date: June 1979
Charts: UK: 9, US: 29, NE: 8, AUS: 18, NZ: 30, GER: 18, SWE: 23
Running time: 54:42

In May 1979, the first fruit of the latest recording sessions – an edited version of 'Night Owl' – was released as a single in Britain, followed closely by the parent album of the same name. This and its predecessor marked the twin peaks of Gerry's career, in chart positions and critical acclaim, even if the second tends to be somewhat overlooked these days. Gerry later claimed in interviews that he was very optimistic when he wrote and recorded it, but in retrospect, he was at something of a crossroads. Having one year earlier delivered an album that had celebrated his release from legal and contractual issues that prevented him from working – the album he'd been longing to make for months – he now found himself writing almost painfully honest songs about freedom, fame, wealth and the wherewithal to do anything he wanted in artistic terms. It was perhaps the best album he ever made. Overall, the sound on the ten rarely-less-than-excellent songs is richer, more lush and a little busier where the backing is concerned but never overdone or cluttered.

But in retrospect, it conveys disturbing messages about the future. At the time, he was on the brink of a struggle with success on an undreamed-of scale, uncharted waters, and most disturbing of all, a drinking problem, which his lyrics sometimes made veiled allusions to. In *Rolling Stone*'s review of *Night Owl* that August, Ken Emerson put a prescient finger on the artist's dilemma. He said Rafferty ought to be sitting on top of the world. 'Instead, he seems to be carrying its weight on his shoulders'.

John Byrne dazzled record buyers with another peerless sleeve illustration, showing an owl carrying a pyjama-clad, guitar-hugging Gerry on its back.

'Days Gone Down' (6:27)

Sometimes referred to less succinctly as 'Days Gone Down (Still Got That Light In Your Eyes)' (the opening line in brackets), this infectious, euphoric number could've hardly given the album a better start. Much of it is a love song: 'We're as much in tune as we were right at the start'. Hugh Burns' rich guitar licks fill in all the right spaces, while warm keyboards and synths, gospel-like backing vocals and an uplifting chorus added all the right ingredients. Though at well over six minutes, it's the album's longest track, it doesn't flag for a second. Only the line 'One more bottle dead and a new day just begun' casts a fleeting shadow. An edited version (3.58) was released as a single in the US (but not at home) and peaked at number 17.

'Night Owl' (6:09)

An equally worthy, if perhaps slightly less commercial single than the foregoing, the title track (edited to 4:24 with a truncated intro and omission of the final verse) gave its creator his second and final top-five hit. Raph plays a solo on the electronic wind instrument the lyricon, at the time a relatively recent invention. The word 'owl' never appears in the lyric, which poignantly portrays the introspection of a character who gets lonely as the sun gets low, having watched himself performing to a large crowd ('One more face in a palace of mirrors') and then found an escape route in 'One more drink' to keep reality at a distance. Some have seen it as a warm, very attractive melody that cloaks an unflattering self-portrait of the artist, conscious of his failings and discomfort in the spotlight, the expectations forced on him by his newfound success, and a tacit recognition of his demons. Be careful what you wish for, indeed. The artist himself plays Polymoog and piano, while Hugh's jangling guitar (like a latter-day Byrds) and Graham Preskett's synthesizer provide an unobtrusive yet colourful backdrop throughout.

'The Way That You Do It' (5:09)

This is another love song, this time expressing gratitude for the guidance from the one who has 'a way of telling me I'm wrong/A way of coming on so strong'. She tells him straight, 'The way that you do it just got to be right', and he wouldn't have dreamed of taking it from anyone else. He's confessing his vulnerability, and she puts him back on the right road. Piano and organ are the main bedrock, the organ evoking some of the more tender moments of the slower cuts on Dylan's *Blonde On Blonde*, while Richard Brunton contributes a marvellous, anguished and pleading guitar solo. Gerry supplements his lead vocal with well-placed call-and-respond phrases.

'Why Won't You Talk To Me?' (3:59)
The third song of a largely confessional nature dwells on a lack of communication. Its theme is the common one of trying to break down the invisible wall between two people wrapped in silence, one desperate to know what's wrong. Why won't the other person talk? Why are they acting this way? Is he supposed to feel guilty? Is he to blame? Everything is set to a sweet, slow 6/8 tempo; John Kirkpatrick's accordion intro is soon joined by Richard Thompson's mandolin, with Hugh Burns' guitar kept in the background, as is a glorious, layered tapestry of Gerry's multitracked backing vocals. This track was also the B-side of 'Night Owl'.

'Get It Right Next Time' (4:39)
A sad song in which the basic question is left unanswered is here, followed by a more resolute one. 'You gotta grow, you gotta learn by your mistakes', 'You gotta die a little every day just to keep awake'. Get it wrong, so you'll get it right next time. Its bright groove in a lively shuffle rhythm, with Fender Rhodes piano and snappy sax break, made it instantly appealing for radio. This was the album's only track released as a single on both sides of the Atlantic, and in each case, it was the second single. It reached number 30 in Britain and number 21 in America. For once, the record company resisted the temptation to edit for the UK 45, though in the US, it lost 50 seconds.

'Take The Money And Run' (5:48)
No matter how veiled, sooner or later, there was bound to be a further reference in song to Gerry's earlier bitter experiences in the music industry. This was written and originally demoed during the *City To City* sessions, as noted above, but he was reluctant to put it on that album, as he said people would think he had a 'money fixation'.

The first version had a brief snatch of synth in the intro. This re-recorded version alters the instrumentation, and to quote Emerson's *Rolling Stone* review, on the intro, 'Ravenscroft's saxophone wails like a bagpipe on a blasted heath'. As far as Gerry was concerned, show business was 'a beast that can chew people up. I took up a certain stance and attitude about my career and wanted to avoid the harsher aspects of it'. In other words, to quote from the lyric, 'Don't trust anyone/Just take the money and run/Buy yourself a place in the sun'. It was inspired 'after Stealers Wheel collapsed into lawyers meetings', though he felt less strongly about it a couple of years later.

At the end of the song comes a whisper from the one that he loved: 'And her heart was saying this can't be right/All my wasted days and her lonely nights'. This rocked much harder than most of the other tracks, with Richard

Brunton adding to the lyric venom on guitar, while the saxophone, accordion and pennywhistle add a touch of the Celtic to excellent effect. The song caught the ear of The Alvin Lee Band, who recorded a more guitar-based version as 'Take The Money' – a single from their 1981 album *Free Fall.*

'Family Tree' (5:57)

Over more than 40 years of creativity, it's arguable that Gerry never wrote a more sublime song than this. Borne from his childhood memories of when the family sang together at home, it later became a favourite that his daughter and the children of his brother Joe sang at family get-togethers. Their live rendition with Barbara Dickson at Gerry's 2012 memorial concert was undoubtedly the highlight of the show.

On *Night Owl*, the intro sounds like a piece of early music, thanks to Richard Harvey's recorders and pipe organ, before Gerry's vocals and acoustic guitar begin. The two Richards – Brunton and Thompson – add electric guitars, with Liam Genockey displaying exemplary drumming restraint in his use of light and shade. Eighty seconds before the end, Richard Brunton's astonishing guitar solo brings everything to a peak before Gerry gently reprises the opening line to an exquisite finish. All in all, it's six achingly beautiful minutes, nothing short of breathtaking.

'Already Gone' (4:55)

Dreams don't last, Gerry mused, pondering having once had one he could lean on, but it's already gone. It's a similar story with the weather, as he waits for the sun to shine, only to find it always rains instead. The next lines are the key: 'I was down, but you changed my luck/And the dream was still the same'. Only love lasts. Here's a gently romantic track cruising along without much drama, and with Richard Thompson's laid-back guitar and Richard Harvey's synth, it makes a pleasant interlude, though it's maybe not the album's finest moment.

'The Tourist' (4:14)

The tourist, in this case, is the musician undertaking a concert tour in America. In view of the fact that his one and only set of dates there never took place after all, it's all rather ironic. There's a sly reference to his being in a baking-hot New York where he 'got the news it just made number one'. A couple of verses later, he sings about being dead on his feet, having 'come a long, long way from Baker Street'. The observant listener will note that he loosely rewrote that from a song on the previous album.

It's taken at the same jaunty pace as 'Get It Right Next Time', propelled with piano and synth and punctuated with a few blasts from Raph's sax. In the concluding lines, Gerry muses that they're ready for anything now: 'Here we go for one more memory/Way back in the 20th century'. As everyone knows, such a tour was the one thing he was not ready for at the time.

'It's Gonna Be A Long Night' (4:24)

There's something of an air of mystery in this lyric. Someone had been out on the loose, and now the small hours have come. There are hints of a haunted man having had a one-night stand with someone who's left her calling card and said her goodbyes, and after that, all he has to look forward to is staring at the moon while he awaits the first light of a new day. This mid-tempo song is given added zest during the breaks featuring piano, mandolin and the guitars of Richard Brunton and Hugh Burns in what comes close to a free-for-all towards the fadeout.

Gerry's elder brother Jim also sought his moment of glory in the spotlight at around the same time. In 1977, Jim was signed to Decca Records, who released his album *Don't Talk Back* and six singles over the next two years. One of them – 'Don't Let Another Day Go By' – secured Jim a new-release slot on *Top Of The Pops* in June 1978. Gerry joined him in the studio as producer and sang backing vocals. But none of Jim's records ever made the charts, though his song 'I See Red' was recorded by ABBA's Frida (Anni-Frid Lyngstad) on her first British solo album and was a top-20 hit in 1982 after ABBA went their separate ways. Ten years later, Gerry recorded 'I See Red' for his *On A Wing And A Prayer* album.

Gerry was now in a position to take stock and do what he wanted at a more measured pace, no longer thirsting for the next top-ten single or album. One of his options was to work with major names. Among those who'd expressed a desire to collaborate with him were Paul McCartney, who sent him a telegram congratulating him on 'an incredible song' after Baker Street'; James Taylor, who wrote Gerry a letter congratulating him on 'Whatever's Written In Your Heart', and Eric Clapton. Gerry said no to all of them, telling Carla that 'Nobody was good enough'. Keenly aware of his musical abilities, he'd proved himself time and time again, and other artists had been covering his songs since his Humblebums days. Yet he still seemed convinced that recording on his own with Hugh Murphy and a selection of musicians who remained part of his semi-official studio roster would give him all he needed. Forming partnerships with others of greater stature would require compromise and would, therefore, possibly mean problems ahead for someone who'd been in duos and bands in the past and was used to doing things on his own terms. Sometimes, the pairing of two major talents is a creative marriage made in heaven; sometimes, it can be a complete train crash.

Carla thought he was just stalling for time. Maybe some new project would suddenly happen, 'But I knew he'd crossed the line as far as the record business went'.

Snakes And Ladders (1980)

Personnel:
Gerry Rafferty: vocals, acoustic guitar
Ian Lynn: keyboards, synthesizer
Billy Livsey: acoustic piano, clavinet, mystery voice, Polymoog, keyboards, pianica
Pete Wingfield: organ, acoustic piano
Bryn Haworth: slide guitar
Jerry Donahue, Richard Brunton: guitar
Mo Foster, Pete Zorn: bass
Liam Genockey: drums
Frank Ricotti: percussion, congas, tambourine, woodblocks
Richard Harvey: pennywhistle
Raphael Ravenscroft: saxophone
Betsy Cook: backing vocals
Chris Mercer: brass arrangements
Will Malone: string and clarinet arrangements
Gavyn Wright: string leader
Produced and engineered by Gerry Rafferty and Bill Murphy
Recorded at Chipping Norton Studios, Oxfordshire; AIR Studios, Montserrat
Record label: United Artists
Release date: April 1980
Chart positions: UK: 15, US: 61, NE: 17, AUS: 31, GER: 34, SWI: 36
Running time: 52:34

Alas, for the contractual demands of being signed to a record company and having to follow up two major successes, both around a year apart. *Snakes And Ladders* was Gerry's fourth solo album, following less than a year later, and there was inevitably a slight drop in quality.

Of the 12 songs, two were remakes of numbers he'd recorded earlier. While there's basically nothing wrong in revisiting and perhaps improving older numbers – especially as they were on albums that sold poorly – it does suggest a whiff of writer's block, understandably considering the pressures he was under.

Moreover, three of the tracks have an element of spoken word from others, two of them being announcements from what we might call a guest ringmaster and the other an extract from a then-recent political speech by a senior minister. The former two sound rather close to novelty, and the latter is an attempt at satire that doesn't quite work. The arrangements and production can otherwise hardly be faulted, though there's a lack of five-star songs.

John Byrne's sleeve design was a clown-like figure somewhat overwhelmed with a giant game of snakes and ladders, sitting against a background consisting of a game board with squares numbered one to 100.

'The Royal Mile' (3:48)

'Farewell sweetheart' is the message of this song in which the troubadour reluctantly takes his leave of the love of his life for a journey south on the night train in pouring rain. Not long before, they'd been walking down the Royal Mile, a street in Edinburgh that Gerry knew very well. An infectious tune, the accordion drone at the start, Scottish drums and pennywhistle make this the most Celtic folk, roots-orientated of his singles. It was the album's only track to be released as a single in America, where it bore the subtitle '(Sweet Darlin')', reaching number 54. It was the second single in Britain, with a peak of 67. In both countries, it would be Gerry's final charting single, excluding a 1990 remix of 'Baker Street', which reached the top 60 in the UK.

'I Was A Boy Scout' (4:14)

Digging even further back into his memories of yesteryear, Gerry muses not so fondly about his formative years. As a boy scout, he had his old patrol, a necktie and a monkey suit. Then what happened? Like so many of his contemporaries, he heard rock 'n' roll, and life was never the same again. Move over, Baden Powell, tell Tchaikovsky the news, here comes Little Richard. In one of the last verses, he mentions his brief shoeshine career again, but now he was 'going into something that was feeling good'. This track could've made another good single, enlivened with Bryn Haworth's slide guitar and Chris Mercer's excellent brass arrangement towards the end.

'Welcome To Hollywood' (5:17)

Welcome to the album's first dose of satire. Gerry delivers a few subtle lyric barbs at the Palm Springs and Hollywood lifestyle in this song, making fun of those who laze around their big house and swimming pool where 'Everybody looks so cool, so bad, so sad' and you're 'Stuck in the middle with the blues again'. Billy Livsey is the star of the show and is worth his weight in gold on piano on this track, also playing Polymoog and other keyboards elsewhere on the album. His voiceovers top-and-tail this track, though one wonders whether exclamations like 'Gerry, love it! Love it! Gerry get down baby!' interjections are better suited to novelty tunes of the Ray Stevens or Guy ('Loving You Has Made Me Bananas') Marks variety.

'Wastin' Away' (3:29)

Love has gone badly wrong here; his 'little darlin'' obviously no longer cares; he's wasting away and getting out. It's the real rocker on this album, with only four additional musicians – namely ex-Fairport Convention member Jerry Donahue on guitar, who lets rip with a masterful solo at the end; Pete Zorn on bass, Frank Ricotti on percussion, and the ever-dependable Liam Genockey giving it everything he's got on drums. He usually sprinkles the rock tunes sparingly, though they always stand out, and this is one of his strongest performances ever recorded.

'Look At The Moon' (2:18)
The album's shortest track is surely its loveliest. With a faintly Randy Newman-esque touch, Gerry goes even more solo than usual, with nothing but piano, restrained synths and strings. It's touchingly simple, almost childlike, with just two brief verses like a little lullaby (one or two more might not have gone amiss). At first, the moon is crying, but by the end, he is smiling: 'He feels just like you'.

'Bring It All Home' (4:40)
The first British single benefited from plenty of exposure on Radio 1 but stalled at a disappointing number 54. Unusually, it finds Gerry in full rolling-blues mode, with a faint nod to the similarly titled 'Bring It On Home To Me'. Gerry sings of being 'Lost on an endless sea' and 'Blind in the light of day', but his loved one brings it all home. Sax is the most prominent instrument, while Livsey's piano, Wingfield's organ and – above all – Donahue's guitar work themselves up into a frenzy. The single was edited to 3:42 and faded early, while the full album version carried on to a spectacular conclusion as Livsey and his keys fell off the metaphorical musical cliff.

'The Garden Of England' (4:08)
A Scotsman who moved to the prosperous South-East of England unleashes his pen as the album's second satirical moment takes a swipe at the generation who remembered their country the way it was not so long before. Where The Kinks' Ray Davies would comment with a little love/hate and gentle but never unkind mockery of a similar mindset in some of his songs (notably on *The Kinks Are The Village Green Preservation Society*), Gerry seems to be turning a fierce eye on those around him who live at home in the garden of England: people who still remember when Britannia ruled the waves. He then fills up the last minute or so with an extract from a speech by then-Home Secretary William Whitelaw on his 'Short, sharp shock' policy, under which young convicted offenders were to be detained in secure units and subjected to firm military discipline. Granted, the speech does sound more like something from the 1950s than 1979. The scheme proved to be an expensive failure and was soon abandoned. Even without the speech, the song was not one of Gerry's better ones: a languid number which couldn't be saved by an elegant but bland string arrangement.

'Johnny's Song' (3:25)
Next are two songs that Gerry had recorded in earlier days. This one, which first appeared on the debut Stealers Wheel album, returns 15 seconds longer due to the fact that it has a similar arrangement but is taken slightly faster. The guitar snarls a little more fiercely here, and between them, Liam and percussionist Frank Ricotti deliver a much stronger rhythm. It comes second only to 'Wastin' Away' as the album's heaviest three minutes.

'Didn't I' (4:14)
This was always considered to be one of the best songs from *Can I Have My Money Back?* Both versions are equally good. Gerry supplies the lead and backing vocals. As expected, the new version is a fraction heavier, with Donahue's guitar more upfront, and lasts about 30 seconds longer, fading out where the earlier one came to a full stop.

'Syncopatin' Sandy' (4:24)
This song drew on memories of Gerry's teenage years in Paisley. He and his friends regularly walked past the town theatre in Smithhills Street on their way back from school. One day, he saw a large poster advertising the pianist Syncopatin' Sandy – a septuagenarian veteran of the old music-hall tradition who used to play non-stop for hours while people came to watch and listen. Among them was young Gerry, who called it one of the most surreal things he'd ever seen. Sandy would sit at his piano for up to a day and a half without stopping while being liberally sustained with whisky. At times he would be playing with one hand and drinking from a paper cup in the other.

It's quite different from anything else on the album. Rhythmically, it marks a return to the good-time vaudeville-esque stomp of 'Mattie's Rag' from *City To City*, or alternatively, The Kinks' 'Dead End Street'. The track is led by piano, with occasional clarinet framing the tune.

'Café Le Cabotin' (4:51)
Le Café Le Cabotin was a restaurant on the island of Montserrat and was owned by Baron de Bon Bon and his wife, Francoise. The Baron's voice can be heard here, welcoming everyone to the establishment. Everyone involved in the making of this album would unwind there between recording sessions, and many a long night was spent in song and knocking back a drink or ten. A story is told of Chianti bottles suspended from the ceiling as decoration. On one occasion, one became dislodged, hit Hugh Murphy and knocked him out for a while. In spite of this, they still recorded a tribute to the place, a sprightly good-time number with Billy Livsey's pianica (a melodica or cross between a harmonica and a small keyboard, sounding like an accordion) being the most prominent instrument. The last minute or so is basically instrumental riffing between pianica and guitar until the fade, and perhaps goes on a little too long, but that's the only fault of one of the most lighthearted tracks here.

'Don't Close The Door' (3:45)
The closing track is primarily a showpiece for Bryn Haworth's slide guitar over some wonderful rippling piano and organ by Pete Wingfield and the rock-solid bass and drums of Pete Zorn and Liam Genockey, respectively. The song is basically a slow, bluesy, lovestruck appeal of a man begging his partner not to close the door and leave him alone for the night. The lyric is

short and doesn't go deep, and the last 80 seconds or so comprises basically the same instrumental phrase repeated until the fade while one longs for the big finish. In short, it's good as far as it goes but is ultimately a little disappointing.

Related Track

'In Transit' (2:55)

The B-side of 'Bring It All Home' sounds like it originated as a studio jam. It might've been left off the album for the reason that it sounds quite out of character and more akin to a one-off union of Status Quo and The Blues Band. But as a final track, it would've completed the record (or a CD reissue) in fine style. To an exhilarating shuffle, Gerry sings about the excitement of air travel – the 747 has just arrived, and everyone's 'sitting or waiting here in transit/Down in no-man's land'. In addition to Paul Pilnick's guitar and Liam's drums, there's also some magnificent blues harmonica that starts early on and really takes flight about two minutes in, shortly before the fadeout. In the absence of adequate personnel information, one can only speculate that it might've been an outtake from *City To City* and that Paul Jones was probably responsible for the harmonica. Jones was asked recently:

> I've had a listen to it, but the harmonica is quite far back in the mix. I certainly have no memory of the session, but that would be true of a good many other sessions at that busy time. From what I can hear, it could be me, and the fact that the producer was (as with *City To City*) Hugh Murphy might strengthen the possibility, but I can't be anything like definite. That's not much help, I know, but I would not claim it myself.

It remained unavailable on CD until its appearance on *United Artistry: The Best Of Gerry Rafferty* – a 16-track, 2017 compilation including mostly A and B-sides from 1977 to 1982, along with Stealers Wheel's 'Stuck In The Middle'.

Lightning never strikes twice, and the momentum created by *City To City* was impossible to sustain. *Night Owl* was less successful, and *Snakes And Ladders* – the third album in three years – failed to reach the UK top ten, while both singles fell short of the top 50. Nevertheless, under the auspices of Ed Bicknell's Damage Management (who also represented Dire Straits), Gerry went out on an 11-date tour of Britain, including shows at London's Royal Albert Hall, Glasgow, Aberdeen, Manchester, Leicester, Sheffield and Swansea in the spring of 1980. The seven-piece Snakes and Ladders band included Julian Littman, Liam Genockey and Raphael Ravenscroft from the 1978 gigs, with Richard Brunton on guitar (a role he'd filled with Rab Noakes two years earlier), Ian Lynn on keyboards, Graham Prescott on violin and keyboards, and Pete Zorn on bass. Richard and Linda Thompson and their band opened each show. Gerry had sung backing vocals on 'Lonely Hearts' from their last album, *Sunnyvista,* released the previous autumn. Going out on the road was part of the job, a limited compromise if not a necessary evil, and while Gerry wasn't against playing live *per se*, he admitted to Colin Irwin his mixed feelings 'about this thing where three or four months of the year you have this whole entourage on tour'.

Gerry had always been a great admirer of the Thompsons' music. Though they'd been much lauded by music critics and fellow artists, following a series of poorly selling albums over the previous five years or so, first on Island and then Chrysalis Records (for whom *Sunnyvista* was the parting shot), they were temporarily without a label. Gerry undertook to provide the finance for the recording of a new album that they could use to obtain a new contract, and as part of the arrangement, he and Hugh Murphy would be co-producers. Accompanied by Pete Zorn on bass and Fairport Convention drummer Dave Mattacks, in June, they recorded some demos at Woodworm Studios and, in September and October, went to Chipping Norton Studios to complete the ten songs they'd chosen. Gerry, Hugh and Linda were pleased with the results, but not so Richard, who greatly preferred the one-take school of recording where possible and felt stifled by Gerry's perfectionist approach and insistence on take after take: 'What worked so well for Gerry – lots of multi-tracking and layering – seemed to work against us. We had fine musicians, but everything was triple-tracked and dense. There was no air in the music. It felt claustrophobic'.

As the sessions continued, Richard felt increasingly excluded from the process. When they reached the mixing stage, he simply didn't bother to turn up because when he said something, he felt he was being totally ignored and consequently thought, 'Hey, whose record is this anyway?'. While admitting that he loved Gerry's records and thought that if just a little bit of the 'Baker Street' magic rubbed off on them, maybe they might get a hit single and, therefore, a top-ten album in its wake, the sessions just didn't work for him. 'Gerry liked to triple-track everything. We'd get three pianos; it became a bit of a Phil Spector issue. Three acoustic guitars, layers and layers of backing vocals, very lush, very evened-out sound'. The end result was nothing like he'd envisaged.

Having invested about £30,000 in the scheme, Gerry kept his word and tried to secure them a deal. But to his surprise, he couldn't find anybody prepared to sign them. It happened at a difficult time when several major labels had just begun to downsize and drop several acts from their rosters, bands and artists who were the darlings of the music press but couldn't sell enough records to chart. A few months later, the Thompsons re-recorded the songs with producer Joe Boyd, whom Richard had known since his Fairport Convention days, and the results subsequently appeared as *Shoot Out The Lights* in 1982 on Boyd's new independent Hannibal label.

The material that Gerry produced – two demos, ten completed tracks and four tracks from a TV performance with Fairport – were left on the shelf until they found their way onto the 1995 bootleg CD *Rafferty's Folly*. In what was probably the last interview he ever gave – to radio presenter and journalist Spencer Leigh – Gerry was surprised to be handed a copy of the record to autograph, as he was unaware the recordings had ever escaped into circulation. Recalling the episode, he agreed that Richard was one of the finest songwriters and guitarists to come out of Britain, while Linda had a beautiful voice, though he found Richard a little wary as it was a bit too slick for his liking. 'I tend to be a perfectionist in the studio, and he wanted something looser'. Gerry conceded that the Boyd-produced album richly deserved the good reviews it received, but even so, unsurprisingly, he added that 'It wasn't a patch on the album we'd done'.

Like Mr. and Mrs. Thompson, Gerry could also feel the blast of cold wind hitting a recession-hit record industry, though in his case, it was more an in-house change of label rather than being left homeless. In 1979, United Artists Records (or rather Liberty/United Artists) was sold to EMI. *Snakes And Ladders* was released on the UA label as it was in its last few months, after which EMI moved the better-selling acts on the roster, including Gerry and also Kenny Rogers, The Stranglers and Whitesnake, while most of the rest, notably The Buzzcocks and The Vapors, were dropped. (As Capitol was, at the time, EMI's main label for releasing American product in the UK, this may help to explain why Gerry's next album was on Liberty and never on Capitol).

At least Michael Gray, the outgoing head of press at UA, was able to find a new job as Gerry's personal manager. Already a well-established freelance writer, Michael had made a name for himself with the book *Song And Dance Man*: one of the first full-length critical studies of Bob Dylan's work. During their three years together, Gray accompanied Gerry when he was working and running his office at Tunbridge Wells. Unlike Brewer, Gray and Gerry hit it off at once. Michael knew that Gerry was very guarded and suspicious of how his talent would be exploited, and Gray soon realised that one of his main jobs was basically to say no to everything.

Sleepwalking (1982)

Personnel:
Gerry Rafferty: vocals, acoustic guitar
Kenny Craddock: acoustic piano, synthesizer, Hammond organ, electric guitar, keyboards, banjo
Alan Clark: acoustic piano, organ, synthesizer
Ian Lynn: synthesizer, sequencer
Hugh Burns, Frank Bogie: guitar
Mo Foster: bass
Liam Genockey, Pick Withers: drums
Christopher Neil: drum programming, backing vocals
Morris Pert, Frank Ricotti: percussion
Mel Collins: saxophone
Produced by Gerry Rafferty and Christopher Neil
Recorded at Chipping Norton Studios, Oxfordshire; Strawberry Studios South, Dorking
Record label: Liberty
Release date: September 1982
Charts: UK: 39, US: did not chart, NE: 26, NOR: 30, AUS: 80
Running time: 37:05

Sleepwalking reached the shops after an interval of more than two years. There was the bare minimum of radio and TV promotion and interviews, and for any future releases, the music was going to do the talking, not the man behind it. Two singles were taken from *Sleepwalking* in Britain, the first being the title track with a non-album B-side, but there was no single in America. It seemed that Liberty were ill-prepared to spend much effort in promoting Gerry if he wasn't ready to make himself available for the purpose.

Changes were immediately evident on his first and only album for the label, which was a shorter LP with only eight tracks, and synthesizers and programming galore as befitted the new musical climate of the 1980s fronted by The Human League, Depeche Mode and others. The more slick, drum machine-heavy production was by Christopher Neil, then best-known for having worked in a similar capacity with Sheena Easton. When Hugh Murphy was interviewed a decade later, he was very matter-of-fact about having been temporarily replaced. Gerry had made three consecutive albums with him, and his debut album long before: 'I think he was pretty jaded at that time, and feeling the pressure, and he just thought 'Well, I'll try another tack', which is understandable'. Also, this time, unlike on the last two albums, no arrangers were credited.

An equally portentous indicator of a new-age Rafferty also came with a mere glance at the album sleeve. Instead of another quirky and individual John Byrne creation (which would also be absent from the next few records), it was a photograph of an empty road and sky beyond, conveying alienation or at least isolation and distancing from everything else around him. The liner notes for the 1989 hits compilation *Right Down The Line* suggested in hindsight that Gerry was at the time 'finding himself at the crossroads and looking to replace the treadmill with a new dimension in his life'.

The general opinion of *Sleepwalking* remains divided, some seeing it as a bold and successful move to another sound, others (this author included) as a new Rafferty trying to keep up with musical trends that didn't really become him, at the same time shedding the charm of the partly acoustic folk rock and rich arrangements that had always been his main calling cards.

According to bassist Mo Foster, only one track was recorded at Chipping Norton before Gerry and the full team moved everything to 10cc's Strawberry Studios South in Dorking, Surrey. The studio was a South-East annexe to the original Strawberry Studios in Stockport, Greater Manchester, that 10cc had built primarily for themselves. The Stockport unit had become so popular with other acts, that 10cc had great difficulty in booking for themselves, hence their conversion of a former Dorking cinema that came up for purchase in 1976.

'Standing At The Gates' (6:51)

The album opens with a lengthy song that, in the absence of interviews and promotion, could be a veiled lyric about Gerry himself, more at odds with the music industry than ever: 'Standing at the gates of a strange new world, like a refugee'. Maybe the key to the song's meaning comes in the last verse: 'Now the spirit doesn't move you/You're so empty, you've got nothin' left to give/ Yes you know by now that nothin' you have ever learned has taught you how to live'. Is he now looking in the mirror at a successful singer who's been catapulted to global fame and fortune without realising it, has the world at his feet, and realises that his career has peaked?

In place of that accommodating folk-rock sound and production, this heralds a hard, colder style. The guitar and organ intro courtesy of Hugh Burns and Kenny Craddock (the latter formerly of the second Lindisfarne lineup) and prominent sax work from Mel Collins impart something of the sound of the last three albums. Even so, it's more funky, less accommodating than Hugh Murphy's production, and thus serves as a warning of rather different musical territory ahead. But unlike some of the other songs, at least it has the benefit of Liam Genockey from the earlier sessions.

'Good Intentions' (4:15)

Enter Chris Neil and the drum programming. The song is the resigned one of a 'sad-eyed dreamer' whose intentions are good. Everyone misunderstands him; life's such a hard school when you're living a lie, and the doctor tells him not to worry about it. It's a rather dispiriting song, not improved by the stark arrangement, which sounds like little more than a demo with Gerry's vocal and a touch of echo on synths, sequencer, and the only acoustic instrument: Alan Clark's piano. Of all the songs here, this is the one that really could've done with a touch of warmth from an acoustic guitar, mandolin or maybe both.

'A Change Of Heart' (4:10)
A rather downbeat lyric drives home the message of living with 'a worried mind and a heart of pain/You drag it around', and in places, it's a rather repetitive lyric. Genockey is back on drums to add the right amount of power, while Frank Bogie's guitar and Kenny Craddock's synths bring some sparkle to what's basically a rather average song. As the second British single, like the title track, it slipped out more or less unnoticed.

'On The Way' (4:24)
The brighter feel of this song gives a feeling of relief and a little *joie de vivre*: 'Light shining down from the east/Bringing a love that won't cease'. There's some happiness at last. A pleasing organ intro leads into a slight calypso feel, Alan Clark's Hammond organ and synths sounding like an accordion, and there's a light touch on the drums from Pick Withers, making two members of Dire Straits together here. The only drawback is more programmed percussion, with a bass synth pattern, faintly redolent of a frog croaking, that soon palls.

'Sleepwalking' (3:51)
The title track and first single included the producer on backing vocals, something he would long remember, as they stood next to each other and he tried to imitate Gerry's nasal intonation, much to the latter's amusement. Neil later recalled, 'I remember him wetting himself laughing; it was hysterical. But it was a big thrill to sing backing vocals with him'.

It's quite a lively track, but the lyric is none too cheerful. He starts out in the street, the rain is falling and he's got nowhere to go. He's bemoaning the state of the music business again, where the beat goes on and on and he's selling his soul to the company man, everybody's on the make and the world's gone crazy. Yet guitar and keyboards combine to produce a strong hook, while the drums add a stirring, funky rhythm throughout.

While it may not be typical Rafferty, it was probably his most successful attempt to deliver a single that fitted with the synth-pop zeitgeist of the early 1980s without trying to jump on the bandwagon and fall flat on his face. But the powers that be on Radio 1 had evidently lost interest, and the single (faded about 20 seconds earlier than the album track) came and went almost unnoticed by the media.

'Cat And Mouse' (5:03)
This is one of those frustrating songs that doesn't seem to lead anywhere. The title appears nowhere, and the lyric says little. In a vague way, it hints at a

lack of communication between two people, with one saying hello and the other having nowhere to run. It might not have mattered if the music was more interesting, but it's just a rather aimless mid-tempo shuffle rhythm, with Clark on synths and Hammond organ and Hugh Burns on guitar, doing their best to enliven what is basically a rather unsatisfactory five minutes.

'The Right Moment' (3:24)

In an in-depth interview with *Folk Roots* six years later, Gerry told Colin Irwin that this was one of his songs that hadn't been heard much, 'but it is the best song I've ever written'. The shortest song on the album, in just two verses, it conveys the message of wasting time 'Spinning on another wheel/Going 'round in slow motion', caught up in a dream when you could be making a better life, just waiting for the right moment. Otherwise, life is just borrowed time and wasting day after day. Like the preceding song, it's relatively short, but this time, Gerry gets to the simple but profound message straight away. Acoustic piano and synths from Clark and Lynn are the only instruments to be heard on what is the most touching song on the record. Olivia Newton-John covered it with full orchestral backing on her 1985 album *Soul Kiss*.

'As Wise As A Serpent' (5:07)

The title comes from the New Testament in which Christ addresses his disciples: 'Behold, I send you forth as sheep in the midst of wolves; be ye therefore wise as serpents and harmless as doves' (Matthew 10:16). It also echoes the previous song in the theme of 'Dreaming our lives away'. It's about holding back and being wary of revealing too much about yourself, as he admits, 'I don't ever hang my soul out on the line'. At last, there's a touch of acoustic guitar, even banjo, and though there are no drums, a haunting synth riff recurs throughout and gives a sense of grandeur. Though it's a slow burner, it is still one of the best songs here.

Related Track

'When I Rest' (3:34)

The B-side to 'Sleepwalking' would probably not have fit on the end of the album any more than 'In Transit' would've on *Snakes And Ladders*. A long way away in spirit from the synths and programming of the preceding tracks, this is a slow, blues-style 6/8 rhythm with Gerry singing his heart out not to be left behind ('Don't leave me here to waste another day'), against piano and drums, while a sax blows a cool jazz flavour.

After *Sleepwalking*, there was an even longer silence when Gerry almost completely stopped creating or at least releasing new music for a few years. Since the success of 'Baker Street', he admitted he'd been touring the world, travelling everywhere and seeing nowhere. Whatever he decided to do in the future, it was going to be at his own pace on his own terms. He said afterwards that he just decided to stop, though he hadn't intended to for quite so long.

> I had quite a hectic period during the *City To City* time, and I decided I wanted to do some travelling. So I did, mainly in Europe and America. We spent nine months in Italy, and then I found myself wondering whether I should do another album.

He had his own recording studio built at the 16th-century Tye Farm near Hartfield, East Sussex, installed electric gates, and worked largely by himself or with Hugh Murphy. Throughout this period, Gerry continued to write, though he released nothing of his own. His sole brief appearance on record around this time was a vocal on 'The Way It Always Starts', a song written by Mark Knopfler as part of the soundtrack for the movie *Local Hero* in 1983. That album peaked at number 14. It was an appropriate pairing, as the Dire Straits frontman had acknowledged Gerry as a major influence on his songwriting, and Knopfler's guitar playing was to feature in some of Gerry's later work.

Four years later, he and Hugh jointly produced The Proclaimers' number-three 1987 hit 'Letter From America': a band version of an acoustic song from their debut album *This Is The Story*. Gerry said, 'They were starting out and had signed a deal with an independent company, who sent me a demo of some songs. They were good, and 'Letter From America' was particularly striking. As a Scotsman, I could relate to a lot of what was being said in the lyrics, and so I did it in my own studio'.

In regard to the absence of any new music of his own, Gerry told Colin Irwin of *Folk Roots* that he enjoyed the chance to live a more normal life and travel outside the confines of his career at last. 'But eventually, my puritanical streak emerged once again, so I settled down, set up a home studio, and started to write and record'.

North And South (1988)

Personnel:
Gerry Rafferty: vocals, keyboards, guitar, bass, acoustic and electric piano, organ, synthesizer, saxophone
Alan Clark, Kenny Craddock: keyboards, synthesizers, Hammond organ
Geraint Watkins: accordion
Betsy Cook: electric piano
Jerry Donahue: guitar
Bryn Haworth: slide guitar
Mo Foster, Pete Zorn, Ian Maidman: bass
Arran Ahmun: drums, percussion
Morris Pert: percussion
Ric Sanders: fiddle
Mel Collins, Andrew White: saxophone
Davy Spillane: Uillean pipes, whistle
Will Malone: string arrangements
Produced by Gerry Rafferty and Hugh Murphy
Recorded at Gerry's home; RAK Studios, London; Odyssey Studios, London
Record label: London (UK), Polydor (US)
Release date: 18 April 1988
Charts: UK: 43, US: did not chart, GER: 20, NE: 23, SWE: 24, SWI: 16
Running time: 56:44

Listening to the first album for almost six years suggests that the sabbatical had allowed Gerry to recharge his artistic batteries. A glance at the personnel list of names like Geraint Watkins, Davy Spillane, and above all, the welcome reappearance of Hugh as co-producer brings expectations of Gerry having returned to form with the promise of the old Celtic magic, especially the prominence of pipes on some tracks. Latin and reggae rhythms also crept in, suggesting another influence that Gerry had soaked up on his overseas travels in his gap years.

In hindsight – as was the case with *Night Owl* – there is a shadow over some of the songs. Titles like 'Tired Of Talking' and 'Hearts Run Dry' and lines saying how all that's left is a pocketful of memories or that a flame is dying suggest a doomed marriage. Others have a world-weariness about being a long way from his roots in Kent, working in London but still yearning to return to Scotland. The use of pipes on several tracks reinforces a strong Celtic thread running through a number of the songs.

The autobiographical title hints – perhaps subconsciously – at the dichotomy between the years Gerry had spent living in and around London and a need to stay in touch with his roots. When Colin Irwin asked him if there was a political undercurrent to it all, reflecting the title phrase in increasingly common usage over the latter years of the Thatcher premiership, Gerry was at pains to avoid undue emphasis on it, admitting that there were a few references. Yet, in a personal aspect it was more connected with the geography of his Scottish birth, yet living at the other end of Britain and travelling regularly between both ends.

Most of the reviews were good, though *The Times*' David Sinclair opined disparagingly that it sounded like Gerry had thumbed a lift up the road to a mock Texan bar somewhere in his native Scotland and that there was 'a mid-Atlantic blandness lurking behind the Rococo-roots veneer'.

Unfortunately, a change of label brought about no more than a modest resurgence of chart fortunes for an album that was a distinct improvement on its successor and deserved so much better. Gerry was still sticking to his guns and letting the music speak for itself, which meant that the album reached the shops with next to no promotional fanfare, hence a modest chart placing at home that indicated a faithful fan base waiting to buy, but little more. It *was*, however, a top-30 album in four European countries. Seven of the ten tracks were over six minutes long, often with unusually long instrumental intros, which probably made it an acquired taste for most radio programmers: that is, the faithful few who didn't regard Gerry as increasingly irrelevant.

The sleeve, credited to World Travel, has another rather stark design, with the artist's name, album title, a compass, and four small photos of skies, vapour trails and a railway track.

'North And South' (6:41)

This song takes as its subject the geographical divide between Scotland, where Gerry was young and ambitious, and London, where he achieved success and realised it was a double-edged sword. As a poor man's son from Scotland who hit the road and followed 'blind ambition', Gerry was attracted to where the days were filled with music and the nights with conversation. A subsequent verse has a veiled reference to the family man and sadness that 'She always wanted so much more than he could give her', having to say goodbye every time he went on the road. Another has a wry reference or even a rhetorical question as to whether his situation is a wilderness or 'Just another station on the Rock Island Line': a nod to the old skiffle song and possibly a metaphor for different stages of his life. There's a lively, bustling rhythm throughout (Celtic funk, anyone?), and the combination of pipes, cutting guitar and saxophone that builds towards the fade works to perfection.

'Moonlight And Gold' (6:10)

Through a remarkable arrangement, this relaxed and richly evocative song sums up an early-morning mood to perfection. The ticking of a bedside alarm clock for the first 20 seconds gives way to a dramatic intro in which strings and ethereal synths complement each other, with a sound not unlike a piccolo out front, before the percussion and Jerry Donahue's picturesque and gentle guitar-playing enter and pave the way for Gerry's vocal almost two minutes in. The full beauty of this song only hits home after several plays, but the references to songbirds greeting the dawn, midsummer magic as the night turns to day, and watching as the moonlight fades combine with the music to capture a perfect mood.

'Tired Of Talking' (4:08)
Surely the most angry song on the record, this one seethes with irritation. Two people are clearly not getting through to each other. He's fed up with talking, so he thinks he'll go out for a walk. It's time they said goodnight and they agree to leave it till the morning. The drums and percussion bristle away fiercely in the background while pipes, pennywhistles and guitars simmer behind the lyric.

'Hearts Run Dry' (6:10)
If 'Tired Of Talking' represented frustration, this one was all about regret and sadness, with an analogy of the setting sun. Here, love grows cold, the young grow old and dreams unfold. The emotion in Gerry's voice is palpable on a wistful countryish ballad sweetened by Geraint Watkins' accordion and, towards the end, Kenny Craddock's Hammond organ. Throughout the rest of the track, there's a welcome edge from Jerry Donahue and Bryn Haworth on guitar and slide guitar respectively.

'A Dangerous Age' (5:27)
The main definitions of that imprecise phrase 'dangerous age' talk vaguely in terms of male menopause, a midlife crisis, behaving recklessly and the like. There's a pointer to this theme here in choice phrases and references to needing to spend time out in the great unknown. All we have is a 'pocketful of memories' and 'code of the road' suggesting that all is not well in the singer's personal life. Gerry's travels with his family are hinted at in a mention of flying away over the mountains, down through the valleys, through the homeland of the Celtic Kings: 'Now it's just the frontline of the USA'. Notice also the plea 'Don't renege on love': 'renege' being an infrequently used word in popular songs. One of the Richard and Linda Thompson outtakes from the 1980 sessions was 'Don't Renege On Our Love'. Coincidence?

Musically, this is definitely one of the strongest songs on an album that has already set the bar high. It begins with a drone combining portentous synths and guitar, giving way to a bustling feel, Hammond organ and other keyboards, a labyrinth of pipes, whistle, and, towards the end, some subtle sax wailing. A short instrumental break halfway through and just before the fade adds an extra twist by entering in a different key altogether.

'Shipyard Town' (6:23)
Though the title appears nowhere in the lyric, Gerry confirmed in an interview with Colin Irwin that the town was Clydebank, where the *Queen*

Mary and the *QE2* were built. It was the home of his wife Carla, whom he first met while playing in his first bands on 'a small town night', and how they married their fortunes together when they 'sealed it with a golden band'. He admitted this was 'an old-fashioned love song', even if 'an exiled heart gets weary'.

Make no mistake, this is a masterpiece. The first minute is a Celtic pipe drone, then it clicks into a shuffle rhythm, with Gerry reminiscing to a tune based on Donahue's Knopfleresque lead guitar.

The basic construction shares another 'Baker Street' characteristic in the subtle shift of key. For the older song's intro and outro in D and the verses in A, read for 'Shipyard Town' after the drone, the intro riff in F#m-A-Bm, and the verses in D, then the outro riff played firstly in the same intro sequence, then the same notes in the key of Bm, and finally as the song fades, another change transposes the notes to the key of Am. All in all, this is Gerry's 1980s Celtic equivalent of 'Baker Street', every bit as fine a piece of work and, to the average listener, all the fresher for not being too familiar or overexposed for its own good. It's ironic that 'Shipyard Town', a song of arguably the same quality, which appeared (minus the minute-long intro) as a single ten years later, was completely neglected upon release. In a better world, a few strategic plays on prime-time national music radio might well have sent its creator back into the stratosphere, even if that may have been the last thing he wanted.

'Winter's Come' (6:28)

Winter is evidently not just a season here but a metaphor for the last long-drawn-out moments of a relationship. Long, cold, lonely nights have arrived, with cold winds, teardrops, broken hearts and talk of moving on. A 40-second intro with an ethereal wash of pipes (this time more like pan pipes than Celtic), followed by a stately guitar with a sweet fiddle in the background, takes us into the song. Two verses and a bridge tell the sad story, then a break allows the guitar and fiddle to breathe a little more, followed by the bridge and a reprise of the first verse in what is one of Gerry's poignant, tender ballads.

'Nothing Ever Happens Down Here' (3:42)

After six minutes of mournful introspection, light relief is on the way. To some, this rockabilly romper might sound like a throwaway, but it comes across as the most fun Gerry's had on record in ages. Amid the lighthearted talk of being stuck at home too long and wanting to start a riot, there are political references – inner city burning, violence on the picket lines, police in riot gear (evidently referring to action during the miners' strike of 1984/1985), and a lady who was not for turning. Accordion, fiddle and guitar turn it into a cajun romp, although, on the minus side, it lacks Liam Genockey or Pick Withers on real drums, which would have been better than the obviously programmed percussion throughout. Even so, it must be the best song Nick Lowe never wrote for Dave Edmunds in the 1980s. It's not the Gerry Rafferty you'd expect, but one wonders whether London Records might've considered this as a single after the failure of 'Shipyard Town'.

'On A Night Like This' (6:11)
Forty seconds of warm acoustic piano notes, followed by almost a minute of accordion before the vocals come in, act as an intro to this relaxed Latin-influenced song. It's another romantic interlude, as Gerry sings of sitting in a crowded room one night, when the room keeps on swaying. Guitar, accordion and a touch of steel drums make for an atmospheric break that takes up the last minute before it fades.

'Unselfish Love' (5:24)
For the last track, we find ourselves in the realms of reggae. In the lyric, he ponders a fancy-free, self-centred youth and what a difference it made to him to discover a woman who could turn his world upside down and keep his feet on solid ground. Keyboards and more Caribbean steel drums provide the backdrop, with Gerry playing saxophone for the first time on one of his records and a guitar break towards the end.

Related Track
'Heart's Desire' (5:41)
Like the similarly-titled 'Hearts Run Dry', the lyric of this 'Shipyard Town' B-side deals with love gone wrong and how 'There's a price to pay for your heart's desire'. Success has cost him dearly in terms of personal happiness: 'Now you've got everything you ever wanted/But money can't buy you a satisfied mind'. Musically, it's the equivalent of mid-tempo soul, with guitar and sax supporting the piano and occasionally taking centre stage.

After the record was released, Gerry told Colin Irwin that for the next album, he was writing songs with the intention of doing something more direct: 'very low-key and sparse, just acoustic instruments, and get away from the very produced sound'. (Physician, heal thyself. For a decade, he'd been his own co-producer). When asked if he had any long-term career plans, he said he was keen to do more production work and get involved with writing a musical. He had various ideas, such as writing something based on the life of Robert Louis Stevenson, a writer Gerry most admired. 'I don't know what form it would take, but something away from the format of ten or eleven songs on an album, which I've done'.

One thing he was adamant about was his determination not to succumb to pressure to come up with anything to match 'Baker Street', even if 'Shipyard Town' was potentially an epic on a similar scale for those who were still listening. He never expected to repeat the success of the earlier song, and it was not in his nature to expect it to happen. 'You've done that; what's the point of trying to do it again?' was his view. 'So I didn't feel any pressure due to it. I was pleased the song drew attention to the album. I was much more pleased with the success of the album than the single'.

Though Stealers Wheel never reformed (at least not with the two main members), in 1989, Joe Egan and Gerry got together at his new home studio at Tye Farm, Hartfield, with Hugh Murphy. They invited Jim Rafferty – who lived nearby in Tunbridge Wells – to join them and complete an unfinished song. By the time Jim arrived, they'd finished the backing track, and Joe, who was responsible for the original idea, had laid down part of the vocal. He was keen for Jim to add to the still partly-developed lyric. After making notes of what they had already done, Joe recorded the full vocal of the song they accordingly named 'Trouble With Love'. Jim then added a distinctive second harmony, followed by a third from Gerry in the closing choruses. Jim said it was great to be in the studio with them and with Hugh, who had always been Gerry's producer except in the Stealers Wheel years. The demo was then put aside and apparently forgotten until Jim came across it over 30 years later on a computer hard drive. He passed it to radio presenter Mike Dillon, who played it on his *Singers And Songwriters* Celtic Music Radio show one evening in June 2022.

Around this time Gerry's health took a turn for the worse, bringing much more crashing down with it. He was bipolar, and episodes such as his sudden departure from and rejoining Stealers Wheel, the personal insecurities that often come with sudden success, followed a few years later by his abrupt cancellation of an American tour at the height of his fame and fortune as a soloist, were a foretaste of things to come. He admitted to periods of depression and said he'd written his best songs during some of his darkest moments: 'For me, singing and writing is very therapeutic. It's much more effective than taking Prozac'.

But his creativity could no longer save him from the enemy in the bottle. In their younger days, when they were less vulnerable, he, Billy Connolly and Rab Noakes had all been heavy drinkers. The latter two stopped before it became too serious, but for Gerry, over-indulgence gradually became alcoholism. During the Chipping Norton sessions for *Night Owl*, the other players and singers realised that one or two drinks too many could make Gerry difficult, and during the Richard and Linda Thompson sessions, Richard discovered that what looked like Gerry's ever-full glass of apple juice *wasn't* apple juice, but whisky. As time went on, Carla found him 'dangerous' at airports and at restaurant tables, where he would lose his temper and scream at her. Occasionally, he would try to put it all behind him and, at his estate, in a mood of renunciation, smash cases of Bordeaux into a stream. Having learned that with alcoholics, 'You should ask them once', Billy noticed once when they met in London in the early 1990s that Gerry was drinking Calvados and had 'about ten or 12 big ones'. An astonished Billy asked, 'Are you okay with your drinking? Do you feel comfortable?' Gerry assured him that it wasn't a problem.

In 1990, Gerry and Carla's marriage ended in divorce. She admitted that there was no hope and would never have left him if there'd been the slightest chance of him recovering. But they were still friends, and she remained ever-supportive, keeping in touch with him until the end.

On A Wing And A Prayer (1992)

Personnel:
Gerry Rafferty: lead vocals, guitar
Paweł Rosak: keyboards, drum and percussion programming
Hugh Burns, Jerry Donahue: guitar
B. J. Cole: pedal steel
Bryn Haworth: guitar, mandolin
Mo Foster: bass
Arran Ahmun: percussion
Mel Collins: baritone and soprano saxes
Joe Egan, Lianne Carroll, Melanie Harrold, Julian Littman, Nicky Moore, Jim Rafferty: backing vocals
Andrew Pryce Jackman: string, bassoon, horn, oboe, brass, cor anglais and arrangements
Gavyn Wright: string leader
Produced by Gerry Rafferty and Hugh Murphy
Recorded at The Farm, Chiddingfold, Surrey; Chipping Norton Studios, Oxfordshire; The Hit Factory; Parkgate Studios, Sussex
Record label: A&M (UK), Polydor (Europe)
Release date: 1992
Charts: UK: 73, US: did not chart, GER: 87
Running time: 57:39

If *North And South* presaged the imminent end of a marriage, *A Wing And A Prayer* confirmed it. *Blood On The Tracks* came to be regarded as Bob Dylan's breakup album, as did *Hand Of Kindness* for Richard Thompson eight years later. Gerry Rafferty's seventh album followed the pattern. It was also notable for a reunion with Joe Egan, who sang backing vocals on eight of the 12 tracks, and for being Gerry's first album to include covers. One was Allen Toussaint's 'Get Out Of My Life Woman', and the other was 'I See Red' by his brother Jim, who also co-wrote two of the songs and sang backing vocals on two others. However, for those who might've hoped for a Celtic thread to run strongly through the songs again, there was no such luck. Even with Hugh Murphy co-producing again, it sounded like the team had tried for a compromise between 1980s and 1990s electropop on one hand and Gerry's Celtic folk-rock inclinations on the other. It's a better album than *Sleepwalking*, mainly because the songs are stronger, but the drum programming threatens to make it sound all too mechanical, if not almost soulless at times. Interestingly, it was the first (and last) of Gerry's albums to appear in Britain on A&M (Stealers Wheel's old UK home), but this album was not released in the US.

'Time's Caught Up On You' (4:21)
With no less than five people on backing vocals – or six if you count Gerry himself – it's a full house on the *a cappella* intro. The lyric sounds like he's

reproaching himself – someone who started out in rock 'n' roll had music deep in his soul but doesn't cut it like he used to do. There are holes in his daydreams that never came true: 'Nobody told you, you reap what you sow'. It all went wrong, but there is reassurance at the end, as eventually he'll 'wake up from this dark night of the soul'. Sax and pedal steel guitar provide some good touches, but overall, it sounds too glossy, and that busy programmed rhythm sounds like too much of a good thing.

'I See Red' (Jim Rafferty) (4:05)
Jim Rafferty released two albums and several singles between 1977 and 1980, but his own version had to wait until 2024 when it appeared as a single on the independent Drag City label. His demo was pitched to Phil Collins, who was producing and playing drums on the first English-language solo album by ABBA's Frida. The song was given an almost reggae arrangement for her album *Something's Going On* in 1982. Clannad also enjoyed a minor (number 81) British hit with the song the following year. Gerry's version is not dissimilar to Frida's, having programmed drums, and contributions on guitar and sax.

The lyric focuses in a veiled way on alienation and modern society, a theme that inspired several of Gerry's songs. The opening line, 'Back in my school days, acting the fool days', talks of a rejection of distancing oneself from military might, or 'Armour-clad horses riding Trojan horses', and survival in a world dominated by the system – an existence in which people should go with the flow and accept what they have. 'Don't we give 'em good TV?'. Reportedly, when once asked what the song was about, Jim said, 'Life in general'.

'It's Easy To Talk' (4:29)
So this is where the main breakup theme begins, with a positively soul-bearing Gerry still desperately in love and pleading to be told where it went wrong. They were living in the city of a million dreams; now he finds, 'You were telling me that love is never what it seems'. The backing is held together mainly by keyboards and strong chords that frame the melody, but pedal steel and slide guitar also help to convey a sense of emotion, even if, again, the drum and percussion programming sounds a little overdone.

'I Could Be Wrong' (3:59)
Doubt and indecision haunt him at every step in this lyric. Their love affair has ended, and now they're just friends. The real thing has gone, but he could be wrong. Day and night, he's been soul-searching in a stormy sea as her tears wash over him. The sadness is gone, but he could be wrong, as he still wants her so much. Which of them is the guilty one? Or are they equally in the dock? The guitar, as ever, is quality personified, but the percussion threatens to suck the emotion out of it.

'Don't Speak Of My Heart' (Gerry and Jim Rafferty) (5:55)
The songs of heartbreak get sadder and better, if that's not a contradiction in terms. Written by both brothers, this finds Gerry pleading his case still more strongly, begging her to take a look at his face, as he still needs, still bleeds: 'I've been running on empty since you went away'. The keyboards and sympathetic guitar fit the mood perfectly, and a string arrangement adds an extra tug at the heartstrings. Mo Foster sat in the studio as he listened to Gerry singing and playing the piano as they arranged this number. He gradually realised that only his fretless bass would provide the right feel for a piece of such powerful emotion, and that what he called 'long growling notes' on the instrument would complement the mood so well.

'Get Out Of My Life Woman' (Toussaint) (4:11)
Then anger takes over. Is it significant that, at this stage, Gerry can't put his fury into words but has to reach for someone else's song instead to convey his wrath? Moreover, the listener is lulled into thinking this could be quite a gentle song after hearing the first 45 seconds: a wailing Celtic take on the intro of his early song 'Her Father Didn't Like Me Anyway'. It's a suitable choice given the circumstances that had inspired Gerry to write that song so many years before. Then comes the surprise – who would've expected him to cover an old song made famous in the 1960s by R&B singer Lee Dorsey? Perhaps even more oddly, the pulsed rhythms and synths sound more like contemporary recent hits from ZZ Top (think 'Legs' and their version of 'Viva Las Vegas'). That said, once you've got over the shock of Gerry making what's almost an out-and-out disco single, it sounds good, even if totally out of character.

It's a pretty uncompromising song, as the sentiments in Toussaint's lyric are obviously anything but charitable – especially the last line '20 long years now I'm black and blue', but Gerry pulls it off just as successfully as The Bee Gees did when they startled everybody in 1975 with their game-changing 'Jive Talkin'', soundwise at least. But if few people took any notice of the album, even fewer were bothered about 'Get Out Of My Life Woman' when it was released as a single.

'Don't Give Up On Me' (4:59)
Far more in keeping with what might've been expected as a 45 in the days when Gerry was the flavour of the month, is the album's loveliest number and surely the finest new song he recorded in the 1990s. The title sets the tone, while picturesque phrases like 'In the dying embers of the midnight hour/All these things brought me misery' and a reference to his stumbling on the road to Calvary all pile on the desolation and sadness more heavily. Bryn Haworth's slide guitar and mandolin – especially when heard together on the break lasting about a minute just before the end – are nothing short of exquisite.

The song achieved some airplay as a particular favourite of BBC presenter Terry Wogan when he hosted the Radio 2 weekday breakfast show but failed to send it into the UK top 100. In Europe it fared better, reaching 51 in Germany and 61 in the Netherlands.

'Hang On' (4:00)
There's a little more positivity to the mood of this one. The message is that when life gets rough, you're in a mess; you hang on or muddle through. (The old Monty Python song 'Always Look On The Bright Side Of Life', expressing similar sentiments that had just been reissued and become a top-three single in Britain, also springs to mind). The more upbeat mood is matched by the music – a faint glimmer of Celtic pipes (or synths emulating the sound) play over a shuffle rhythm, powered by saxes in what might be seen as a close relation to 'Get It Right Next Time'.

'Love And Affection' (6:25)
The longest track on the album remembers the good times, looking at the past through rose-coloured spectacles. They gazed down deep into a wishing well; the sun shone every day and 'Rain seems constant now' as they met like strangers on a lost highway. A smooth number with some attractive melodic touches and a middle-of-the-road arrangement, it's rather bland, dominated instrumentally by gentle piano, lush strings, horn and oboe. While the credits list Hugh Burns on guitar, he's so far down in the mix as to be barely audible.

'Does He Know What He's Taken On?' (4:56)
There's no trace of love or affection to be found here, let alone any wishes of good luck towards his ex's new love. Gerry never *did* growling, but he comes close to it as he muses how his successor will manage: 'He sees your beauty, but I know your needs'. To a mid-tempo rock beat, Jerry Donahue and Bryn Haworth battle it out on guitars, while Mel Collins' sax joins the fray from about halfway through, with a tidy little instrumental wind-down as it fades out.

'The Light Of Love' (Gerry and Jim Rafferty) (4:57)
The second fraternal co-write follows in much the same vein as 'Love And Affection', though lyrically it lacks the same sadness. It's just as sentimental but more positive, despite the line 'Saying all those last goodbyes'. He observes that love is 'like an elemental tune that never dies'. The guitar can be heard much better this time, and the arrangement of strings, brass and cor anglais provide a magnificent garnish, although the melody is not one of the strongest.

'Life Goes On' (5:22)
After the sadness of some of the preceding songs, the record ends on a more upbeat note. It brings the message that life will get better and hearts will mend: 'In that moment when your dreams are scattered in the dust/You find

something you can trust', and later, 'In that moment when you know you might have given up/Someone fills your lovin' cup'.

At the end of the 1980s, when asked if he had any plans to go back on the road, Gerry said he was considering a few dates at the Edinburgh Festival, and if it worked out well, he might play more elsewhere, 'But the performing thing has never been a great need in me'. However, he had come to terms with the importance and necessity of live work. In February and March 1993, he made a brief return to the concert hall for the first time in over 12 years, with dates in Antwerp, Utrecht, Hamburg, Edinburgh, Glasgow, Nottingham, Manchester, and finally, the Hammersmith Odeon in London. These were the last shows he ever played.

No official recordings were released, but the Edinburgh Playhouse gig was recorded for BBC Radio, and almost an hour's worth was later broadcast, while the complete set of the German performance subsequently appeared on the bootleg CD *Live At The Music Hall, Hamburg*. The 17 songs on the latter included nothing from before 1972, the oldest being the Stealers Wheel numbers 'Late Again' and 'Stuck in the Middle', followed by a selection from his solo career and the covers 'Get Out Of My Life Woman', The Band's 'It Makes No Difference', and as an encore, Elvis Presley's 1960 track 'Mess Of Blues' (revived some two decades later by Status Quo), given a new dimension thanks to a soulful vocal and a powerful break shared by sax and organ. Among the ten-piece band were Hugh Burns and Jerry Donahue on guitars, Pete Zorn on bass, Mel Collins on sax, Kenny Craddock on keyboards, and Liam Genockey on drums: all of whom had appeared on some of Gerry's recent albums.

Over My Head (1994)

Personnel:
Gerry Rafferty: acoustic guitar, vocals
Arran Ahmun: drums, percussion
Bryn Haworth: guitar, mandolin
Paweł Rosak: piano, keyboards, bass, harmonica, marimba
Mo Foster, Pete Zorn: bass
Rab Noakes: guitar
Mel Collins: tenor and baritone saxophone
Ian Lynn: keyboards, synthesizer, string conductor
Julian Dawson: harmonica
Lianne Carroll, Nicky Moore: backing vocals
Brad Dawson: shaker
Produced by Gerry Rafferty and Hugh Murphy
Recorded at Tye Farm, Hartfield
Record label: Polydor
Release date: 1994
Running time: 50:39
Charts: did not chart anywhere

Only seven of these 13 tracks were written by Gerry on his own, with four of them re-recordings of past glories, although at least one is arguably a marked improvement on the original. Sadly, this was to be the final album with Hugh Murphy. It was also Gerry's first since the 1971 debut with Transatlantic that failed to chart anywhere.

'Bajan Moon' (4:27)
A relaxed Caribbean flavour opens the album, as Gerry sings about being under the starry skies by the light of a Bajan (or Barbadian) Moon, with the sounds of the ocean and a moonlit sea and a hint of romance in store. The synths and subtle slide guitar breathe an atmosphere of the West Indies, bookended by a wash of tropical sound effects. He'd already begun to explore world music influences on *North And South*, and this is an interesting continuation of the same.

'The Waters Of Forgetfulness' (3:40)
A slapped bass riff, a funky rhythm, synth brass effects and jazz-flavoured tenor and baritone sax set the mood for a number that seems to have its origins in Greek mythology. The theme of the lyric seems to be the river Lethe in Hades and how those who drank from it would forget everything. It may be an analogy for 'drinking to forget', something the writer might have pondered in the aftermath of the end of his marriage. The opening lines mention being lost in a dream with no memory remaining. After a night of sleeping comes a day of gazing into the waters of oblivion or forgetfulness.

As a voracious reader, Gerry might've come across the 18th-century story by James Ridley about Sadak, a mythical character sent to find the waters of oblivion, immortalised in a popular 19th-century painting by the Romantic artist John Martin, which also could've been an inspiration.

'Down And Out' (5:49)
Gerry had written so many songs about himself and his stormy relationship with the music business that it comes as something of a surprise to find a song with a story, maybe about two fictitious characters. A woman 'let a good man down' after meeting a younger man and going to live with him in Germany. Then he (which one is left to the listener to guess) drifted from town to town and went to live in Mexico. The narrative isn't taken any further. Musically, it's a good tune, slightly let down by an overly busy programmed rhythm track, but with attractive backing vocals and, best of all, some fine dobro playing.

'Over My Head' (2:48)
This first of four old songs from his back catalogue was originally on *Ferguslie Park*. The arrangement here is basically the same, but the more colourful instrumentation (organ piano, dramatic lead guitar and strings) of the original is replaced by synths, which simply don't do it justice.

'The Girl's Got No Confidence' (2:51)
Another story song, this tells of an intelligent young woman who's got money, good looks, beautiful clothes and a law degree and who has read the Gurdjieff books and pioneered the introduction of the CD is now sitting pretty, living uptown, but has no confidence. One suggestion online would have us believe it's partly about Linda Thompson. It's also the most catchy song on the album by a mile, with a tune that registers straight away.

'Wrong Thinking' (Egan) 3.54
Maybe Gerry should've called on his former musical partner a few years earlier, for Joe's contribution is one of the strongest songs in the collection. It follows much the same introspective path as some of the songs on the final Stealers Wheel album – 'wrong thinking', letting things get out of hand, being overly critical of others, and the like. But again, it's such a commercial and infectious song that, at first, you hardly notice the downbeat lyric matter. Add slide guitar, mandolin, and colourful Bruce Hornsby-esque piano, and it's a sheer delight.

'Lonesome Polecat' (de Paul/Mercer) (5:25)
This old show tune from *Seven Brides For Seven Brothers* (one of the songs that the Rafferty brothers grew up with as children) was regularly shared with Rab Noakes at Tunbridge Wells while Stealers Wheel was being

formed. It may be a sad song, but still one to listen to with a smile on one's face. Piano, synths, slide guitar, harmonica and a soft touch on the drums bring it gently up to date.

'Right Or Wrong' (Egan/Rafferty) (4:20)
'Right Or Wrong' Mk II sounds much more powerful than the first version that graced the album of the same name. In the ensuing years, Gerry had brought the key down from G to E. But what really makes the difference is that instead of the predominant acoustic guitar, strings and, in particular, the first violin solo, is the fact that now it really rocks. It's taken at a slightly faster speed, with electric rhythm and slide guitar and an additional bridge about halfway through. It manages to be about 20 seconds shorter than the original 1975 take. Finally, if you substituted Mick Jagger for Gerry on vocals, it could almost be an outtake from the Rolling Stones' *Exile On Main St.*

'Late Again' (Egan/Rafferty) (3:50)
The simple charm of this song has never faded throughout the years. Again, the key has been dropped, from B to G. Apart from a longer intro, which means the vocals come in later, and thus a song which is almost 40 seconds longer this time around, it follows the old arrangement very closely, so when it comes to choosing a preference, there's really nothing between either.

'Clear Day' (Egan/Noakes/Rafferty) (3:12)
Rab Noakes recorded this song on *Red Pump Special* in 1974, with Gerry and Joe on backing vocals, and released it as a single. Twenty years later, Gerry claimed it for himself. Rather like the preceding song, it's very simple but delightful in its optimistic message about waking up in the morning, the fog having lifted, like a folk-rock version of Johnny Nash's 'I Can See Clearly Now' in fact. Rab's recording was a minor classic of its kind, and Gerry can hardly improve on it but certainly does it justice, with the added bonus of mandolin and acoustic guitar.

'Out Of The Blue' (Lennon) (3:33)
The original appeared on John Lennon's 1973 album *Mind Games* as a song he'd written to Yoko Ono for his gratitude to her for having come to him at a time of profound misery in his life. Ironically, he recorded it just as he and Yoko were on the point of separating, though they reconciled about a year later. All his life had been 'a long slow knife'. Gerry's version follows the arrangement of the original faithfully, albeit in a lower key. Whose version is superior is a matter of opinion, depending on whether the listener prefers the vocal style of the man from Liverpool who wrote it or the man from Paisley. However, the former didn't have the benefit of Bryn Haworth's excellent slide guitar work, which evokes something of a George Harrison feel.

'A New Beginning' (4.10)
Lyrically, this could almost be 'Clear Day' continued, with its message of seeing everything in a new way, living in a new world, and going down a different road. A slightly funky rhythm with an intro, a harmonica interlude and snatches of complementary lead guitar add a pleasant touch.

'Her Father Didn't Like Me Anyway' (2:40)
The song that originally graced Gerry's first album when he was half of The Humblebums always remained one of his proudest achievements. He dropped the key when re-recording it: now in G instead of A. Accompanied only by piano and acoustic guitar and without the woodwind interludes, it loses almost two minutes in length but remains a touching, bittersweet postscript to a relationship. There is added poignancy when we remember that Gerry and Carla – whose father cared little for him – were married soon after the original was released. By the time he recorded it again, they'd been divorced for four years.

Though Gerry's new albums were now only selling to a faithful fan base, his back catalogue was about to have a belated surge of chart success at home. A selection including 14 of his solo tracks alongside two Stealers Wheel hits – *One More Dream: The Very Best Of Gerry Rafferty* – was released in October 1995 on the PolyGram TV label. Supported by strong advertising, it entered the UK album chart at 17 and spent over six months there. His only compilation to become a hit in Britain, it earned him his first gold disc since *Night Owl*.

In the latter part of his life, Gerry had an unfortunate tendency to make headlines, especially in the tabloids, for the wrong reasons. His brother Joe passed away in 1995, and Hugh Murphy's death from cancer in 1998 – ending a professional partnership that had endured for almost 30 years – was another severe blow. The loss of the men left Gerry deeply depressed, and he became even more of a recluse. Relations deteriorated between him and his surviving brother Jim, who set up the website Effing Peasants, apparently after an insult Joe claimed was directed by his brother against him and his friends. Further taunts, such as The Human Bottlebank and The Great Gutsby, and allegations that he surrounded himself only with yes men, were bandied about online by the elder sibling. It's a sad story, especially considering their collaborations of only a few years before. Even so, there would be two further albums during Gerry's lifetime.

Another World (2000)

Personnel:
Gerry Rafferty: vocals, acoustic guitar, synthesizer, bass, keyboards, piano, Fender Rhodes
Giles Twigg: guitar, bass, drums, percussion, reading
Mel Collins: saxophone
Arran Ahmun, Dave Suttle: percussion
Cindy Legall, Tamara Marshall, Karen Griffiths: backing vocals
Bryn Haworth: guitar, mandolin
Julian Littman: guitar, accordion, backing vocals
Kenny Craddock: keyboards, accordion, Hammond organ
Mark Knopfler: guitar
Vic Linton: guitar
Mo Foster, Pino Palladino: bass
Ronnie Rehse: German reading
Produced by Gerry Rafferty
Recorded at Chipping Norton Studios, Oxfordshire
Record labels, release dates, running times: Icon (online), 2000, 66:09; Hypertension (CD), 2003, 70:44
Charts: GER: 78

At the dawn of the new millennium came *Another World*. Originally available only through Gerry's website as a download, it was later issued on CD on the Hypertension label. Having lost his co-producer Hugh Murphy, he was now producing himself with the aid of an engineer.

With an increased interest in mysticism, he was also exploring church music, gospel, world music and African tribal rhythms, in the process moving a little further away from the folk-rock territory he'd generally been associated with. Mark Knopfler appears throughout the album on rhythm guitar and lead guitar.

The Hypertension reissue had a slightly amended track order, with 'La Fenêtre' replaced by 'Keep It To Yourself'.

'All Souls' (5:20)

The opening track reveals a very new Gerry Rafferty, light years from anything you've ever heard him do before. The message is a battle cry from 'all souls in the wilderness', a vision of a world with no compassion, a mindless society of 'sex, celebrity and fashion' in which he's ill at ease or 'in too deep'. Maybe the approaching millennium and the sense of being on the precipice of a brave (or unknown) new world had some influence on his consideration of where he and the rest of society were going. Musically it's best described as a fusion of soul, gospel and funk in the backing vocals, with a nod to hard-rock territory in the gritty guitar work, with a touch of African tribal rhythms.

'Land Of The Chosen Few' (5:13)

In the lyric, we sense something of a hymn, the words portraying a world of dreams where everyone is a restless spirit, a refugee on the planet Purgatory, searching for the Promised Land and, with it, a new world of peace and harmony. The gospel thread still runs through in the mid-tempo chant structure.

'Keep It To Yourself' (5:42)

One of Gerry's personal favourites from the songs he'd recorded in the Humblebums days on *Open Up The Door*, this is over two minutes longer, extended by more instrumental work with the saxophone and a loose, jazz-like shuffle rhythm on the drums.

'Sweet Love' (4:27)

As Gerry said of 'Shipyard Town', 'Sweet Love' is basically an old-fashioned love song, but minus the distinctive Celtic qualities of the former. Pleasant, undemanding, unadventurous, with a smooth backing of mainly organ and programmed percussion, with restrained little guitar phrases here and there, it sounds like the kind of song Al Green and others of his ilk might've sung. Gerry even does a convincing soul-like falsetto near the end.

'Whose House Is It Anyway?' (Rafferty/Littman) (4:31)

Co-written with Julian Littman, one of Gerry's regular backing singers, this begins with a voiceover in Italian. In an interview with Janice Forsyth on BBC Radio Scotland in 2003, Gerry mentioned that it came about as a tongue-in-cheek commentary on celebrity culture, inspired by a party at a large house in Rome one night where he found himself rubbing shoulders with people from the fashion world, film industry and music business. (Is there a pattern emerging here, seeing as how his first major hit was also a satire written after attending a showbiz jolly?) The reference to seeing Bob Dylan singing for the Pope came about when he returned to his hotel afterwards and saw Dylan on the TV dressed like a cowboy giving a concert in Vatican Square. After changing channels, he saw an elderly Pope who looked as if he was asleep in his chair, and Gerry was immediately struck by what he thought was a hilarious juxtaposition of the two men.

'It's Better This Way' (4:00)

The album's second song of great romance is a lament for a lover in America, ending with hope for a brighter future: 'Tomorrow we'll walk in the sun'. Taken at a gentle pace, with organ prominent in the backing, it sounds reminiscent of late-1970s Dylan.

'Conscious Love' (4:26)

Speaking of whom, this also has strong echoes of Dylan from his *Slow Train Coming* phase. There's a slow, funk mood with pungent guitar phrasing and a touch of gospel-flavoured backing vocals. So many modern panaceas – sex, drugs, money, medicine, potions, friends – won't heal sickness, is the message. Only knowledge, understanding, and, above all, conscious love, can. Then follows a short list of spiritual and cultural icons – among them Abraham, Moses, Jesus, Buddha, Gurdjieff, Socrates, Plato, Rembrandt, Leonardo da Vinci, Rumi, Hafiz, Marcus Aurelius and Johann Sebastian Bach.

'Sweet Surrender' (4:02)
'Got to see the man who won't beat around' goes the second line of this uncharacteristically funky song, loaded with programmed percussion and keyboard chord stabs. There seems to be a spiritual message in saving oneself, one day at a time.

'La Fenêtre' (3:17)
This track was only included on the original online version of the album but later replaced by 'Keep It To Yourself'. Gerry sings in French, the translation of which reads basically about two lovers waking up and looking out the window at another world: the world of their future. It's a lively Cajun romp with a strong rhythm and has accordion and mandolin to the fore.

'Everytime I Wake Up' (5.52)
Like many other people at the time, Gerry looked into the abyss as the millennium approached. This song was his harsh view of the future – the Information Superhighway changing everyone's life at a stroke. 'I'm living in a different world/So much useless information meant to stultify my mind' is his verdict. The intro is a ripple of electronic sound, with a short reading by Ronnie Rehse from a monologue by Austrian poet Rilke. Synthesized strings and the warmer sounds of an organ provide the backing, eventually joined by saxophone and the reading of a passage by Giles Twigg from *Digital Delirium*: a book about ethics and digital reality.

'Xavier & Honor' (3:10)
Following an uncompromising look into a strange new world comes this touching lullaby written for the children of John Byrne and actress Tilda Swinton. A dreamy pattern of synthesizer music evoking a childlike world is overlain with the comforting story of two youngsters for whom a special star shone in the sky when they were born. They live in a world where they can walk through the fields in the sun and gaze at the stars all night.

'You Put Something Better Inside Of Me' (Rafferty/Egan) (4:52)
In revisiting one of his favourite songs from the Stealers Wheel era, this gained just over a minute in playing time, but something was definitely lost. When heard alongside the original, it shows how much harsher his voice seems to have become over the years. There are a few alterations – where the

original (in the key of A throughout) begins with Gerry and Joe singing the title; here, there's a short intro of synth and a sung line, another new line about three minutes in, and after that, a change of key from F to B. Having multi-tracked the vocals, the harmonies are still exquisite, and he's also added a few curves to the melody, but not to advantage, and the more-gospel backing vocals that appear in the last minute are rather overpowering. All credit is due to Gerry for revisiting his back catalogue almost 30 years later, but whereas 'Late Again' from *Over My Head* had been hardly altered at all and still sounded excellent, here some of the original's beauty was removed in the process.

'Metanoia' (3:24)

Metanoia is Greek for 'Changing your mind', and here it gives a title to a song of Christian imagery. There's a religious slant from the opening lines: 'My father's mansion has many rooms/But we all live on the lowest floor'. It's a gospel song set to a reggae rhythm with bubbling organ and the much-repeated refrain: 'We sing a song of repentance, a song of joy'. Yet again, Gerry seems to have taken Dylan as his vocal role model.

'Children Of The Sun' (4:04)

A sweet church organ serves as the intro. Once again, the Christian theme is paramount – in its message, the human race is not as one: 'We are legion, we are many'. We are all children of the sun, lost and alone in a dry desert without a trace of water, crying in the wilderness beneath the sun. One moment, it's straight gospel, and the next, there's a touch of reggae, while Gerry's vocal alternates with a call-and-response routine from the backing singers.

'Another World' (10:40)

To close the album, the title track finds Gerry questioning his partner about whether there's a reason on Earth to believe in him after all the times they've been through, and if there's just one thing left that she sees in him, he will give her his love. Here's a very spiritual dimension, in that if they should meet in another world, he will recognise her soul. The song is like a wistful hymn, backed largely by organ. Then, the fun begins. It fades out by 4:30, to be followed by a short gap and then the first hidden track - a female, spoken incantation over acoustic guitar and synth until 5:49. After four minutes of silence comes a second hidden piece: a jokey ditty, 'Goodnight Mrs. Grinch'. Neither of these are referenced in the accompanying booklet.

By the end of the 1990s, new technology provided Gerry with a way to distance himself even further from the conventional approach of the music industry and work entirely on his own terms. Now, he could bypass the most unpleasant aspects of it and put his work online. As he explained in a press release in November 2000, 'My heart and soul have gone into this album, and by releasing it in this way, my creative influence has not been diluted in any way'. Thanks to the internet, it seemed he no longer needed the old promotional machinery to sell himself and could take his craft straight to an appreciative public. He felt he had matured as an artist, telling the *Evening Standard* that he'd reached the stage where he no longer wanted to be talking to 23-year-old record executives who were just trying to sell their products to 19-year-olds. 'I'm older and my audience is older. They'll know where to find me'. He revealed that the entire record had been made for about £200,000, with half spent on travel, the recording system costing £75,000, and the website and marketing adding £25,000.

Now based in London, and with Hugh Murphy no longer present, Gerry employed sound engineer Giles Twigg to assemble a Digidesign mobile recording studio. With Twiggs' help, Gerry recorded *Another World* in London, Scotland, Barbados, France and Italy, using collaborators from previous albums, including Hugh Burns, Mark Knopfler, Kenny Craddock and Mo Foster. It was initially available only from his company Icon Music, through which he promoted and sold the album independently on his website www.gerryrafferty.com, created specifically for the purpose. In 2003, the album appeared on the Hypertension label, featuring another album cover by John Byrne.

Gerry's enthusiasm for this new approach to recording and marketing continued for the next three years. In a blog post dated 31 March 2004, he wrote, 'Let's get back to music. After all, that's the only reason that this website has been set up'. Gerry held steadfast to his new system and was content to let his music enter the marketplace almost unnoticed except by dedicated fans, who had by then long given up on the then-current singles and album charts. Another posting online announced that he intended to release his work regularly as free downloads, and if he wanted to, he could put a new track out every two weeks or so. However, only a few songs were ever released this way, and the website closed down without explanation not long afterwards.

Sadly, this wouldn't just be the era of a new approach to his music but also the era of lurid stories in the tabloid press about him spending time in California and flying back to Britain or Ireland, being helped off the plane drunk, checking into five-star hotels, drunkenly abusing staff and leaving his accommodation in such a state that soiled furniture, bed linen and carpeting had to be disposed of, and the room completely cleaned and refurbished. One senior manager said he was a very likeable, unassuming man when sober, but after a few drinks, it was another story. One such stay came to an abrupt end when Gerry was taken to hospital to be treated for liver problems and then vanished into the night, leaving his clothes and luggage behind him. For a while, he lived in Ireland, where flashes of the younger Gerry resurfaced. Walking into a pub one evening in West Cork, he delighted punters by taking musical requests well into the night.

At around this time, he met Enzina Fuschini, an Italian designer who was his companion for a while. She reportedly put considerable efforts into helping him to turn his life around.

Life Goes On (2009)

Personnel:
(As for new tracks only. The remainder are as for the three previous albums.)
Gerry Rafferty: vocals, programming
Andy Patterson: bells, engineering, programming
Giles Twigg: percussion, engineering
Produced by Hugh Murphy and Gerry Rafferty
Recorded at Tye Farm, Chiddingfold; Icon Studios, East Sussex; The Hit Factory, London; Chipping Norton Studios, Oxfordshire; Studio Miraval, France; Blue Wave Studios, St Philip, Barbados; Parkgate Studios, Sussex; Skibo Castle, Dornoch, Sutherland, Scotland
Record label: Hypertension
Release date: November 2009
Running time: 77:19
Charts: did not chart anywhere

By 2009, Gerry was in better physical shape. Having recovered to some extent, he was urged to issue a statement, saying that he was alive and well, living in Tuscany and preparing a new album. It later emerged that all this time, he had still been still in England, living in the West Country. At intervals, he'd continued to write and record what would be his last album during his lifetime.

Most of the six new edits are slightly shorter than the originals on the three previous albums and, in some cases, fade out a little sooner. 'The Waters Of Forgetfulness' is the exception, this time gaining about 70 seconds thanks to a haunting new introduction.

Timings in brackets below are the length of the original versions. The others are basically unchanged.

'Kyrie Eleison' (Mozart) 3:50
On the first of the six new tracks, a church bell tolls three times, leading into a religious chant from the Catholic Mass. Multi-tracked, Gerry sings it as a round, creating a choral sound, interspersed part-way through with 'Lord have mercy, Christ have mercy'. This was evidently an echo of the routines of his Catholic school days.

'The Waters Of Forgetfulness' (New edit) 4.53 (3:40)
'Don't Speak Of My Heart' (Gerry Rafferty/Jim Rafferty) 5:58

'Because' (Lennon/McCartney) 2.47
A faithful re-creation of one of The Beatles' songs from the *Abbey Road* album, and according to John Lennon, inspired by listening to Beethoven's 'Moonlight Sonata'. Gerry's version faithfully follows the Beatles arrangement, with similar multi-tracked vocals.

'Everytime I Wake Up' (New edit) 5:20 (5:52)
'Love And Affection' (New edit) 5:57 (6:25)
'The Land Of The Chosen Few' (New edit) 4.00 (5:13)
'Life Goes On' (New edit) 3:06 (5:22)
'Another World' (New edit) 3:52 (4:30)
'Time's Caught Up On You' (New edit) 3:51 (4:21)
'Conscious Love' 4:28
'Over My Head' 2:50
'Hang On' 4:00
'It's Easy To Talk' 4:29

'The Maid Of Culmore' (Traditional) 4:08
An old Irish ballad thought to date from the late 1800s, this was the kind of song that Gerry and his brothers would've been brought up on in childhood and would've probably heard around the Scottish folk clubs.

'Your Heart's Desire' 5:45
This was originally a non-album B-side of 'Shipyard Town' in 1988 (notice minor difference in the title), with minor remixing here where lead guitar and sax are concerned. Despite that, there's little to choose between both versions.

'Adeste Fidelis' (Traditional) 4:08
As at the start of the album, the bell tolls three times. It's as if we've come through a full journey of Gerry's secular music and now arrived at the threshold of Christmas. Multi-tracked again, Gerry the choir (and programmed organ) sing 'O Come, All Ye Faithful' in Latin.

'Silent Night' (Gruber/Mohr) 3:30
To round off the collection comes an equally reverential rendition of the early 19th-century carol, with Gerry providing the programmed brass accompaniment.

According to press reports, Gerry and Enzina were engaged on Christmas Eve 2009. By this time, his health was deteriorating, and the following year, he was increasingly unwell. In November 2010, he was admitted to the Royal Bournemouth Hospital, where he was diagnosed with multiple organ failure and placed on a life-support machine. At one point, he wasn't expected to live for more than a few hours. Having always sworn that he'd never die in hospital, he rallied sufficiently to be discharged and return to Stroud, Gloucestershire, with Martha and her daughter Celia at their home. They all knew it would be his last Christmas.

A few days later, Martha realised the end was approaching, and she immediately contacted some of those who'd been closest to him over the years. Rab came south to say goodbye and share a few songs that had been part of their shared soundtrack. When he got to 'Lonesome Polecat', Gerry sat up a little and sang along gently. John Patrick Byrne also made the journey from Edinburgh to Stroud so he could spend a few final hours with his old friend. Billy Connolly was in Australia when given the sad impending news, so he said his farewell with a few text messages about past memories, which had both of them helpless with laughter: Gerry as much as he was able.

Gerry died on 4 January 2011, aged 63, leaving an estate valued at £1,747,802, reduced after liabilities to a net total of £1,248,524. As he'd made his will in 2007 and left it unaltered, Martha and Celia were the sole beneficiaries. He was cremated at Woodside Crematorium in Paisley, and his ashes were scattered on Iona. Among the 400 who joined the family at his funeral at St Mirin's Cathedral in Paisley were Rab Noakes, Barbara Dickson, The Proclaimers, Graham Lyle, the First Minister for Scotland Alex Salmond and several Members of the Scottish Parliament. During the service, John Byrne delivered a eulogy. Martha, her cousins and the three sons and two daughters of Gerry's late brother Joe sang an *a cappella* version of 'Whatever's Written In Your Heart', which they'd previously sung at home as children and which seemed perfect for the occasion.

After the ceremony, Martha and Rab jointly agreed that the best tribute possible would be a concert of his songs in Glasgow, and Celtic Connections undertook to stage it at the Royal Concert Hall as one of their key events the following January, one year after his death. Tickets sold out so quickly that a second show was added.

Stephen Dalton's review in *The Times* praised 'this warm-hearted communal celebration', with special mentions of Jack Bruce, who turned 'Shipyard Town' 'into a rising blast of Tartan-clad faux-Bruce Springsteen', and Paul Brady, whose 'Baker Street' 'once a byword for drive-time radio naffness, packed a real emotional punch in a boisterous five-guitar arrangement'. Brady was a good choice for the song, as *City To City* had inspired him to change his own musical direction by writing and arranging his own material. He said that when he heard the album, 'I decided to say farewell to traditional folk music and see if I could become a songwriter'.

Extracts from the concert were televised, as was the TV documentary *Right Down The Line* with contributions from family and those who'd worked closely with Gerry. Among them was Billy Connolly, who broke down on camera as he recalled that even during Gerry's last day or so, they 'laughed right up until the very end, but he knew it was time to go and he went'.

Rest In Blue (2021)

Personnel:
Gerry Rafferty: vocals, guitar, percussion
Katie Kissoon: vocals
Rab Noakes: backing vocals
Hugh Burns, Frank Bogie, Richard Brunton: guitar
Bryn Haworth: guitar, slide guitar
Alan Clark, Kenny Craddock, Tommy Eyre, Graham Prescott, Pawel Rosak: piano, keyboards, Hammond organ
Mo Foster, John Giblin: bass
Liam Genockey: drums
Scott Bryant, Kirsty Main, Colin Mackey, Daniel Pioro, Maria Turowska, Abigail Young: violin
Rebecca Lesan, Cameron Smith: cello
Nico Ersfeld, Samuel Omalyev: viola
Andy Patterson: bass, tenor guitar, mandolin, percussion, vocals
Mark Pusey: drums
Mark Rafferty: harmonica
Martha Rafferty: percussion
Produced by Martha Rafferty and Rudy Tambala
Record label: Parlophone
Release date: September 2021
Charts: UK: 73, US: did not chart, SWI: 63
Running time: 63:24

It came as no surprise that the one-man band had continued to work in his home studio, adding to his archive of demos, some of which were recorded as far back as the early-1970s. Despite an air of finality about some aspects of *Life Goes On*, Gerry was actively planning to follow it with yet another collection of material recorded during the last four or five years of his life. Martha was aware of some of the songs he intended for it, and after his death, she knew that, at some point, she owed it to him to return to what he'd started and see if she could bring it to fruition.

A year after he passed away, she put her own home studio together and invited Andy Patterson – not only the engineer but an accomplished musician himself – to help her work on the songs. As Andy had begun working on the album with Gerry around 2006, at some stages coming to work daily until about eight months before his death, he'd been there from the start. Some of the musicians Gerry had worked with over the years remembered recording various parts of the tracks. Once Andy arrived, Martha realised it was too soon and she wasn't emotionally ready for such a personal labour of love. The lockdown during the Coronavirus pandemic (which began in spring 2020), which almost coincided with the tenth anniversary of Gerry's death, 'was the key to everything'.

Once Martha entered the studio with recordings in various stages of completion, she realised that the first part of the process was for her to remove some of the multi-layered synths he'd added to the songs so that his voice stood out more clearly. What she really wanted was for the album to reflect to some extent what she'd grown up hearing – basically, his voice with guitar or piano and with as little extra accompaniment as possible. 'That's the real test of a person's talent, and it was just so beautiful. Everyone who has heard him like that realises how great he was, and I really wanted to try and capture that'. Nevertheless, once she'd pasted together the best parts – sometimes recorded several years apart – she and Andy called in Hugh Burns, Bryn Haworth and Alan Clark, session singer Katie Kissoon and London-based producer Tambala, along with other players and singers as required. Even a few musicians who had long since passed away – including Tommy Eyre and Kenny Craddock – had played on some of the demos and thus posthumously took their due place in the credits.

The cover design was also ready to go. Following a regular tradition that had begun in 1969, a painting by John Byrne (from about 30 years earlier) was used. Gerry had bought it and always intended to use it as an album cover. Thus, it adorned this record.

'Still In Denial' (3:02)

A simple greeting of 'Good morning' at the start becomes an unflinchingly honest song that he evidently wrote for – or rather to – himself and the problem he wouldn't admit, the habit he couldn't kick: alcoholism. 'You're still in denial', he tells himself. Given our knowledge of his life, it's a sad song, and it comes across with anger, growling out his words against a hard-hitting backing track of slide guitar, harmonica and organ. Martha admitted he was under no illusions about what he was, feeling in some ways that he'd inherited the disease from his father, that it was his way of coping with the bipolar disorder, being in and out of detox several times.

'Full Moon' (5:26)

The slower track two is directed more at Gerry's anxieties about mental health. To quote Martha again, being bipolar and suffering from recurring depression triggered his lifelong alcohol problem. To a bluesy piano-and-guitar-oriented tune that ends with a solo calling to mind the likes of blues guitarist Gary Moore (who died a month after Gerry, his last years also dominated by a severe drink problem), this song pleads with the doctor for some salvation for a man whose soul is lost and whose mind is sick, fighting against a battle he can't win, like a full moon on the wane.

'Sign Of The Times' (3:31)

The anger's still burning bright, but this time against the issue of climate change. It's in the form of a wake-up call, warning those living in a dream world that nothing's going to stop the hurricane, those who don't even know that something's wrong and are living in the here and now. The urgency of the subject matter is matched by some blazing guitar and organ work, culminating in another colourful solo and frenetic drumming to match.

'You Are All I Want' (4:44)
Love songs don't come much more tender than this. It has a lightly-picked acoustic guitar, with a tender synth-strings arrangement that embellishes the melody and his voice as he savours the moment that 'I knew my heart had found a home'. A sweet little guitar solo brings it to a perfect finish.

'I Still Love You' (4:07)
A glorious wash of organ that could've almost come from Dylan's *Blonde On Blonde* (and we might say the same of Gerry's impassioned vocal) introduces us to another charming, simple song of love and devotion.

'Wild Mountain Thyme' (McPeake) (4:51)
Sometimes known as 'Purple Heather' or 'Will Ye Go, Lassie', this must be one of the most-recorded Scottish/Irish folk songs of all time. Gerry sings it here against acoustic guitar with the most sparing touch of piano. Martha was keen to include it on the album as she said it was the one tune that would've touched the heartstrings of people who knew him well, and they would probably have heard him singing it and similar traditional numbers at parties and gatherings. When Billy Connolly heard the recording, he admitted it brought a tear to his eye.

'Slow Down' (4:53)
Like the first two tracks, this lyric might be addressed to the writer himself. It comes across as a gentle plea to a friend to slow down and not take it all so seriously, and 'Soon you will awaken to a brighter day'. A more funky rhythm from guitar and drums temporarily makes space about two-thirds of the way through for some startling whooshing sounds on guitar and synthesizer.

'It's Just The Motion' (Thompson) (5:47)
This was one of the songs Gerry and Hugh co-produced with Richard and Linda Thompson in 1980, which they re-recorded for their subsequent album *Shoot Out The Lights*. Accompanied by piano and the lightest of touches from acoustic and lead guitar and rhythm section, Gerry delivers a superb, heartfelt treatment of this song of reassurance in troubled times, ending on the positive note that 'It's only the pain that's keeping you sane, and gives you a mind to travel on'.

'Look At Me Now' (5:20)
Gerry returns to soul ballad mode, with his voice straining slightly on the higher, almost falsetto notes. It's another love song, this time about romance

slipping away. A slow 12/8 rhythm is emphasised by organ and little stabs of electric guitar to add extra bite.

'Dirty Old Town' (McColl) (5:35)
This much-recorded contemporary folk favourite is sung slowly to emphasise the lyric's stark picture of romance in an industrial Salford. Gerry turns it into a country-blues lament with restrained slide guitar, organ, bowed bass and plaintive harmonica to add to the character.

'Lost Highway' (4:38)
Watching TV coverage of Operation Desert Storm during the Gulf War at the start of the 1990s brought home to Gerry the futility of how the modern world was standing still while 'We still kill each other'. Sounding like American country rock, it's an interesting melody, much of it over minor chords, with slide guitar and harmonica providing most of the backing.

'Keeper Of My Soul' (4:00)
A bitter song about the aftermath of his marriage, this lyric dwells on how, having thought his love for his wife Carla would never end, she left him for another man. In spite of that, she still needs to feel control, and has told a friend she was the keeper of his soul. Musically, it goes even further into country-rock territory, with a laid-back backing of slide guitar, organ and female backing vocals, with a pronounced vibe of Bonnie Raitt about it.

'Precious Memories' (3:56)
A gospel song sometimes credited to J. B. F. Wright in the 1920s and sometimes given as 'traditional' by the numerous artists who have recorded it (including Johnny Cash, Willie Nelson, Aretha Franklin and Bob Dylan), this is a solo piece for Gerry, where he accompanies himself on a gentle acoustic guitar. One can well understand Martha's comments saying when his more-folky recordings were stripped of the excess production, the timbre of his voice suited songs like this to perfection.

'Stuck In The Middle With You' (Egan/Rafferty) (3:36)
'Right, here we go', Gerry announces at the start. In a sense, this final (so far) album takes us back to where we came in, with the song that initially made him and his band a household name. Martha remarked that it was 'really nice to hear him singing that song with a mature voice'. The key of the song has dropped from D to C, but otherwise it follows the original very closely. Bass guitar, drums and handclaps come in at the same time, though there are minor differences in the slide guitar. He manages to restrain himself until after the final chord, when he breaks down in raucous laughter, as does another voice off-mic: presumably the engineer. Having a good-humoured reprise of the first hit makes for an excellent way to end.

Anthologies

Gerry Rafferty's early recordings have appeared on several CD anthologies. The really essential one, *Who Knows What The Day May Bring* (Grapefruit/Cherry Red, 2019), gathers the 18 Humblebums tracks on the first disc and 24 on the second, 13 of them comprising the complete *Can I Have My Money Back?* album plus an orphan B-side, 'So Bad Thinking', alongside demos and alternative versions.

The world still awaits a complete box set of all the material recorded from 1977 to date, should such a release ever become possible. *Gerry Rafferty & Stealers Wheel Collected* (Universal, 2011) is three CDs comprising 54 tracks and is the most comprehensive – the first two discs with 32 tracks from his solo career 1977-1994 onwards (one of them the collaboration with Mark Knopfler), while the third disc comprises 13 songs from the Transatlantic years, solo and with The Humblebums, plus eight from the Stealers Wheel albums.

United Artistry (Varese Sarabande/Rhino, 2017) consists of 16 tracks, mostly from the United Artists years, as the title suggests, including both orphan B-sides, all bookended by Stealers Wheel's 'Stuck In The Middle' and Gerry's first Liberty A-side 'Sleepwalking'.

For Stealers Wheel, look no further than *The A&M Years* (Caroline, 2017), a box set with all three albums on CD in miniature facsimile sleeves, plus the bonus on disc one of three tracks recorded for the BBC in December 1971, thought to be the only sessions still surviving. As far as the A&M material goes, it's complete except for the original single version of 'Everything Will Turn Out Fine'. The *Ferguslie Park* re-recording remains the default one used by compilers over the years.

Gerry Rafferty Remembered

Celtic Connections, Royal Concert Hall, Glasgow, 22 January 2012
Band: Roddy Hart And The Lonesome Fire, with Mel Collins (sax), Hugh Burns (guitar), Graham Prescott (violin), Betsy Cook and Barbara Dickson (backing vocals)

Songs performed at the tribute concert (not in order):
Jack Bruce – 'Shipyard Town'
Rab Noakes, Martha Rafferty – 'Can I Have My Money Back?'
Rab Noakes – 'Moonlight And Gold'
Paul Brady – 'Baker Street', 'One Drink Down'
Emma Pollock, Rab Noakes, Martha Rafferty – 'To Each And Everyone'
James Vincent McMorrow – 'My Singing Bird'
Roddy Hart – 'Her Father Didn't Like Me Anyway'
Mark Rafferty, Rab Noakes – 'Mary Skeffington'
Emma Pollock, Rab Noakes – 'Late Again'
The Proclaimers – 'Mattie's Rag', 'City To City'
Barbara Dickson – 'As Wise As A Serpent'

Ron Sexsmith, Emma Pollard and Betsy Cook – 'Right Down The Line', 'Days Gone Down'
Jack Bruce, James Vincent McMorrow – 'Waiting For The Day'
Jack Bruce, Tom Robinson – 'Life Goes On'
Tom Robinson – 'Get It Right Next Time'
Family (Martha, Claire, Mark, Neal, Brian, Eileen Rafferty) – 'Family Tree' (with Barbara Dickson), 'The Ark', 'Whatever's Written In Your Heart'
All (Encore) – 'Stuck In The Middle With You'

What Became Of The Others?

If one of The Humblebums went on to become the man generally acclaimed as Scotland's greatest singer-songwriter, there's a pleasing symmetry in that the other one came to be known as one of Scotland's – if not Britain's – all-time greatest stand-up comics. Billy Connolly had several strings to his bow, and his subsequent career has also encompassed movie acting in comic and straight roles, writing plays and memoirs, and presenting TV documentaries. As a solo recording artist (comedy, music and a combination of both), from 1974 in the UK, he had 11 hit albums, two reaching the top ten, and four top 40 singles, the first and easily the most successful being a parody of Tammy Wynette's 'D.I.V.O.R.C.E.', hitting number one in 1975. Billy was awarded the CBE in 2003 and a knighthood in 2017 for services to entertainment and charity.

Tam (Tommy) Harvey left the music business and died in 2021, aged 78.

Joe Egan released two albums, both produced by David Courtney, who had co-written and co-produced Leo Sayer's early work. *Out Of Nowhere* (1979) contained the two singles 'Back On The Road' and 'Freeze'. Among the musicians involved, were Benny Gallagher, Graham Lyle, Alan Parker, Henry Spinetti and ex-Stealers Wheel member Paul Pilnick, the latter on guitar and bass. Some of the songs – all written by Joe – partly reflected the troubled times Joe went through during the Wheel days. *Map* (1981), released in the US as *Stay As You Are* in 1982, featured some songs written entirely by Joe, some collaborations with Courtney, and Joe's own version of The Everly Brothers' 'The Price Of Love'. On both records, his style was very similar to that of Gerry. *Map* received little attention, and Joe then ran a music publishing business from his home in Renfrewshire. *Out Of Nowhere* was released on CD by Angel Air in 2016. He died in 2024, aged 77.

Rab (Robert) Noakes went on to make over 20 solo albums on various labels, including one on Ringo Starr's shortlived Ring'O Records. He remained a much-respected name on the Scottish music scene, even though national chart success always eluded him. Later, he also worked as a BBC music producer and was a member of the Musicians Union executive committee. Remaining active almost to the end, he died in 2022, aged 75.

John Patrick Byrne was renowned not only for his art, several of Gerry's album covers and the design on his acoustic guitar, but also as a playwright and author of two BBC drama series: *Tutti Frutti* and *Your Cheatin' Heart*. He died in 2023, aged 83.

Others On Gerry Rafferty

Gerry was a scream. He used to have me on the floor. Any time anybody saw him, he was straight-faced, playing these beautiful songs, great melodies he'd composed. They'd never think he was capable of this. I was privileged to have spent my formative years working with him, and there remained a strong bond of friendship between us that lasted until his untimely death. He had extraordinary gifts, and his premature passing deprives the world of a true genius.
Billy Connolly

The success from 1978 onwards was phenomenal. He reunited with Hugh and made some exceptional records. As an artist and producer, he knew what he wanted from people, but he also knew how to leave space for them to make their own marks. He could never be described as shallow, and I have benefitted from and enjoyed his generosity of spirit. He had little patience with lazy living. He was over-reliant on received wisdom and sloppy thinking, and his patience was tested as much as anything did.
Rab Noakes

He had a lot of ideas of how he wanted the songs to go, but basically we got free rein to do what we wanted to do. And if he didn't like something or he wanted to change something, he'd make suggestions. But from a musical point of view, I thought he was great to work with. And every time he played you a new song, the hairs on the back of your neck went up because he was brilliant as a writer. He was the most amazing artist I have ever worked with.
Gary Taylor, bass guitarist on the *City To City* sessions.

'Baker Street' was about how uncomfortable he felt in the star system, and it was a giant world hit. The album *City To City* went to number one in America, and suddenly, he found that as a result of his protest, he was a bigger star than ever. And he now had more of what he didn't like. Although he had a few more hit singles in the United States, by 1980, it was basically all over, and when I say *it*, I mean basically his career because he just was not comfortable with this.
Paul Gambaccini, BBC Radio 1 and 2 presenter.

I feel extremely close to Gerry, and his memory lives deep in my heart. So, without getting too metaphysical, I still feel connected to him and feel that he's very close to me. At first, I thought it would be inappropriate to hijack his career, but after further consideration, I realised it wouldn't be hijacking; it would be creating an album to help people connect with Gerry and his music. It's actually like saying, 'He's not gone because his music remains'. Many people only know 'Baker Street' and 'Right Down The Line'. They have

little idea of the depth and breadth of his music, so I thought an album could widen the appreciation of Gerry's talent.
Barbara Dickson, about recording *To Each And Everyone – The Songs Of Gerry Rafferty.*

He doesn't use a lot of fancy poetic terms; he doesn't cloak what he's saying in mystic mumbo jumbo. He gets to the point, and I think almost uniquely, you could listen to the songs down the years and connect them with what you later find out was going on with his private life.
Tom Robinson

I've always been a big Gerry Rafferty fan. I heard the song 'Right Down The Line' come on the radio a few years ago, and the guitar came to me like a lightning bolt. Gerry was such a soulful and unique artist, and I'm very sorry he passed before he could hear our version of his song.
Bonnie Raitt

I think Gerry Rafferty was one of the few people who really successfully straddled the worlds of both folk and popular music. He did it really well, and he was respected in both camps.
Charlie Reid, The Proclaimers.

He didn't know how good he was. He was one of the most talented musicians and singers I ever knew, but he completely underestimated his own talent. He was a very humble man.
Finbar Furey

His legacy lives on. The saxophone piece from 'Baker Street' has been thumping in my head all of my life.
Alex Salmond, former First Minister of Scotland, at Gerry's funeral.

Resources

Books

Connolly, B., *Tall Tails And Wee Stories* (Two Roads, 2019)
Dickson, B., *A Shirt Box Full Of Songs: The Autobiography* (Hachette, 2009)
Emerick, G. and Massey, G., *Here, There And Everywhere: My Life Recording The Music Of The Beatles* (Gotham, 2006)
Garner, K., *The Peel Sessions* (BBC, 2007)
Stephenson, P., *Billy* [Connolly] (HarperCollins, 2001)

Articles And Interviews

Bacon, T., 'City To City (Live review)' (*Sound International*, August 1978)
Beattie, E., 'Long-lost Stealers Wheel track rediscovered by Gerry Rafferty's brother' (*Scottish Daily Express*, 14 June 2022)
Chandler, A., ''Baker Street': The Mystery of Rock's Greatest Sax Riff' (*The Atlantic*, 17 December 2015)
Clarke, S., 'So what about that Beatles influence?' (*New Musical Express*, 20 June 1973)
Dadomo, G., 'Stealers Wheel – for real' (*Record Mirror*, late 1973)
Dellar, F., 'The Producers: Hugh Murphy' (*Sound International*, November 1978)
DeMain, B., 'Gerry Rafferty, 'Baker Street', and the sax intro that gave birth to an urban legend' (*Classic Rock*, 4 August 2022)
Docherty, G., 'Billy Connolly breaks down during tribute to his old pal Gerry Rafferty' (*Express*, 23 August 2011)
Drysdale, N., 'How a song by The Beatles brought Gerry Rafferty and Rab Noakes together' (*The Courier, Evening Telegraph*, 18 May 2021)
Emerson, K., 'Gerry Rafferty's 'Baker Street' Blues' (*Rolling Stone,* 24 August 1978)
Heathcote, C., 'Gerry Rafferty is back on a new platform' (*Sunday Express,* 22 November 2009)
Irwin, C., 'A Humble One' (*Folk Roots*, 1988); 'The man who was down to earth' (*Melody Maker*, 12 May 1979)
Leigh, S., 'The Right Moments: Gerry Rafferty' (*Record Collector*, February 2011)
Means, A., 'Humblebums – a change has got to come' (*Melody Maker*, 25 July 1970)
Page, M.F., 'Join up the jigsaw and you have the Wheel' (*Sounds*, 15 March 1975)
Plummer, M., 'Can I have my voltage back?' (*Melody Maker*, 30 November 1971); 'Why Wheel went off the tracks' (*Melody Maker*, 7 July 1973)
Rees, D., 'Night Owl' (*Classic Rock*, February 2018)
Rowley, S., 'Gerry Rafferty: The Man Who Hated the Music Business' (*Classic Rock*, 4 January 2019)
Sexton, P., 'Gerry Rafferty: bipolar alcoholic, industry misfit, one of Britain's most treasured musicians' (*Independent,* 31 August 2021)

Telford, R., 'Gerry wants to be taken on face value' (*Sounds,* 27 March 1971)
Wavell, S., 'Getting there by tube (Gerry Rafferty got off the gravy train…)' (*Guardian*, 19 July 1978)
Young, A., 'Rafferty's £1.7m estate' (*Daily Mail*, 16 October 2011)
https://www.theatlantic.com/entertainment/archive/2015/12/baker-street-gerry-rafferty-saxophone/421008/
https://web.archive.org/web/20110715165702/http://www.redstone-tech.com/gerry_bsb/folk_roots_1988.htm

Journals And newspapers

Classic Rock
Daily Mail
Daily Telegraph
Disc And Music Echo
Express
Guardian
Melody Maker
New Musical Express
Record Collector
Record Mirror
Rolling Stone
Sounds
The Times
Zigzag

Internet

45cat.com vinyl database
allmusic.com
Discogs.com
gerryrafferty.com
songfacts.com
stealerswheel.com
ukrockfestivals.com
vintagerock.com

TV

Right Down The Line documentary, 59 minutes, first shown BBC 2, 29 August 2011 – available on YouTube at time of writing.

Would you like to write for Sonicbond Publishing?

At Sonicbond Publishing we are always on the look-out for authors, particularly for our two main series:

On Track. Mixing fact with in depth analysis, the On Track series examines the work of a particular musical artist or group. All genres are considered from easy listening and jazz to 60s soul to 90s pop, via rock and metal.

On Screen. This series looks at the world of film and television. Subjects considered include directors, actors and writers, as well as entire television and film series. As with the On Track series, we balance fact with analysis.

While professional writing experience would, of course, be an advantage the most important qualification is to have real enthusiasm and knowledge of your subject. First-time authors are welcomed, but the ability to write well in English is essential.

Sonicbond Publishing has distribution throughout Europe and North America, and all books are also published in E-book form. Authors will be paid a royalty based on sales of their book.

Further details are available from www.sonicbondpublishing.co.uk. To contact us, complete the contact form there or
email info@sonicbondpublishing.co.uk